LORD TED

The Dexter Enigma

LORD TED

The Dexter Enigma

Alan Lee

GOLLANCZ/WITHERBY

LONDON

First published in Great Britain 1995 by
Gollancz/Witherby
A Division of the Cassell group
Wellington House, 125–130 Strand, London WC2R 0BB

Unless otherwise stated, all
photographs are reproduced
courtesy of Allsport.

A catalogue record for this book is
available from the British Library.

ISBN 0 85493 245 3

Photoset in Great Britain by
Rowland Phototypesetting Ltd
Bury St Edmunds, Suffolk
Printed and bound in Great Britain by
Butler and Tanner Ltd, Frome, Somerset

Author's Note

For all the attention that has attached itself to him throughout his life, Ted Dexter is an essentially private man, as this book will emphasize. It could not, therefore, have been written without the generous assistance of a number of people and I am especially indebted to Douglas Birks and Michael Martin for their help in reconstructing Ted's schooldays at Radley. Others who gave freely of their time and memories were Richie Benaud, Sir Colin Cowdrey, Ossie Wheatley, Alan Smith, John Woodcock, Robin Marlar, Mike Smith, John Snow, Alan Oakman, Ray Illingworth, David Gower, Graham Gooch and Michael Atherton. I am grateful to them all, and, of course, to Ted himself.

Prologue

It was an appropriate image. The classically drawn features were blurred behind the glass of the Edgbaston committee balcony but the expression was unmistakably grim, the eyes revealingly weary. Ted Dexter was surrounded by people but, as so often, alone with his thoughts as he sat watching the England team – by association, *his* England team – heading for one more defeat in a year of relentless purgatory. It was to be the last one he would suffer.

For more than four years, Dexter had been testing out his theory that life had prepared him for the job as overseer of England's cricketing fortunes. Much had been achieved, great strides taken towards the establishment of an infrastructure designed for a richer future. This was of little account to the majority, whose concerns began and ended with the bottom line of current Test results. England, after an embarrassing winter in the subcontinent, were now being trounced by Australia. It was the third Ashes series since Dexter became chairman of the England committee and all had produced the same, melancholy outcome. Dexter could not survive this one and he knew it. What is more, as he gazed bleakly across the Birmingham ground towards the press box awaiting his remains with scarcely concealed impatience, he no longer wanted to survive.

This was August 1993 and, after much soul-searching and no little intrigue, one England captain had just given way to another. It might have been a comfortably appropriate time for Dexter to hand over, too, but there was nothing comfortable about the circumstances in which he found himself. His dignity, on which many believed the Dexter image relied, had been undermined by

7

events, assumptions and what the following year's *Wisden* was to call the 'doltishly brutal abuse in the tabloid press'. Worse, the security of his position had been eroded from within, by a group of county chairmen who had long resented his influence and were now not above allying themselves with the most scurrilous of newspapers in order to oust him. At the next meeting of the Test and County Cricket Board, certain of those men were themselves witheringly condemned and humiliated by a colleague of greater stature and, clearly, greater principle. It was too late to salvage Dexter his dignity, much less the job he had relished with such boyish enthusiasm.

Dexter's demise was greeted with glee by some, with sadness and anger by others. Yet few, precious few, genuinely knew what Dexter himself felt about it. He chose, typically, to keep his own counsel, to bear whatever injustices he perceived had been thrust upon him in a silence that did him credit. A little more of such silence, at sensitive moments, might indeed have avoided such an outcome, for it had been Dexter's singular sense of humour, expressed as light wit or sarcasm yet wilfully translated as solemn statement of fact, that had brought him into terminal conflict with much of the media and, by inference, the cricketing public, rendering his chairman's seat untenable.

Of course, he had made other mistakes. What chairman of selectors has not? The prolonged omission of David Gower is the one issue for which many will never forgive him; the selection of young players, such as Mark Lathwell, at the wrong times, and of older ones, such as John Emburey, when past their sell-by date, will also be cited at length. But maybe his greatest error was in distancing himself from team matters, giving his manager and his captains too much power. The hands-off approach, leaving him freer to concentrate on the many other, less obvious matters within his brief, was admirable in conception but fraught in practice. When the train left the rails, as it did with a dreadful clatter in 1993, Dexter would still be accountable for every failing, and any credit for other achievements would be conveniently overlooked.

If this was how it was to end, how Ted Dexter's career in cricket would be remembered, what tragically short memories we all have. The man was a rare and compelling batsman, as brave and exciting as they come; an unorthodox, infuriating yet sometimes visionary captain, the first to conquer one-day cricket. He was also a good man, though many would have it otherwise.

Accessibility is all, when it comes to sporting heroes. Dexter's character is inaccessible, by his personal wish; *ergo*, he is glibly misunderstood and unthinkingly dismissed as an eccentric. Few know anything about him. Yet, comfortingly, evidence that his spirit had survived the latest fall was plain in the summer of 1994. Dexter came to the Lord's Test against South Africa. There, he could be spotted, eyes ablaze with the animation of an incurable theorist, gripping an imaginary bat, feet apart in imaginary stance and showing a small gathering of friends how some batsman or other could improve his game. This was pure Dexter. This was how he should be remembered.

Chapter One

He never was an ordinary boy. Time and familiarity can cloud the memory, confuse the mind, but it is the commonly held opinion of those qualified to judge that Edward Ralph Dexter was always, well, different. Even when barely out of short trousers, it is said, he conducted himself with a style way beyond his years and displayed such a breadth of natural talents, and with such ease, that he became the subject of admiration and envy in equal measure. His manner, later to be condemned by some as haughty, even contemptuous, was at school regarded by his peers as imposing, and by his elders and masters as impressively singular. To one and all, it marked him out as the leader of men which, in many diverse ways, he has been all his life despite, beneath that deceptive veneer, possessing a personality which was not cut out for command.

This paradox will recur throughout the story, for the general acceptance, in whatever environment he has found himself, is that Dexter will take charge. This has been justified by his presence, usually by his ability, but countermanded by something within him. Misjudged and maligned down the years, for an approach that lacks the common touch, Dexter has frequently been thought aloof and uncommunicative. In truth, he is simply shy.

The shyness has manifested itself in various ways, notably a vagueness known to irritate and infuriate. Its genesis, however, is an unease in company. Dexter has innumerable acquaintances, and always has had, but he is genuinely close to few. Perhaps this can be traced back to that period of his childhood when he was essentially rootless. In rapid succession, he attended prep schools in all four countries of the United Kingdom, yet still spoke with the accent, and probably behaved with the ways, of his Italian infancy. Enough, surely, to confuse the most organized young mind, let alone one already subject to whimsy.

The nomadic nature of Dexter's upbringing was due, more than anything, to the uncertainties of that time. He was born on 15 May 1935, and when war was declared on Hitler's Nazis, Dexter was a serenely unaware four-year-old, whose crawling and toddling time had been spent among the privileges, if not the pampering, of a rich family with two desirable homes in the Italian sunshine. Transported, of necessity, to the safer haven of Britain, Dexter had to start his schooldays with the world in turmoil and his own family no longer sure if, or where, either home or business existed.

Ted's father, Ralph Marshall Dexter, was an active, outgoing man, distinguished of features and with wavy, silver hair. He was also extremely prosperous. Between the wars, he had set up his own underwriting agency in Milan. It became known as Bevington Assicurazione and its success was founded on the fact that the major British insurance companies were forbidden to trade in Italy. In time, Dexter acquired agreements to conduct the Italian affairs of such giants as Commercial Union, Eagle Star and Royal. Commercially, his cup ranneth over, and in family life, too, he and his wife, Elise Genevieve, were to be blessed.

Elise had three daughters, Ted's half-sisters, from a previous marriage and she and Ralph had three sons. The first-born was John, two years Ted's senior and a mirror image in many ways. Some years after Ted's birth came the third son, David, and it was here that sadness struck a family otherwise touched by fortune. David was a Down's syndrome child but, unlike so many, he survived, and survives still. For many years now, he has lived in a Care Home, his needs provided for by his elder brothers.

Because their ages were so close, their abilities similar, John and Ted were destined to take an identical course through academia. After prep school came Radley, followed by Jesus College,

Cambridge. A generation earlier, Ralph Dexter and his two brothers had also studied simultaneously at the same Cambridge college. Doubtless, he was properly proud of his sons, their progress and popularity, but he was not often on hand to tell them so. In the war he served with distinction in the RAF and, when hostilities ended, he returned to Italy where, somewhat to his surprise, the homes and business were intact and ready for resumption.

The boys, though, were to stay in Britain for their education, seeing their parents only in school holidays and on occasional weekend visits. Such enforced independence was not peculiar to them, of course, but in their case its effect was to mould strength and character early in life.

It was not always easy for them. If ever they could be accused of the silver spoon, for instance, it certainly did not extend to the prep school they attended in Scotland, where their difficulty in understanding the locals was apparently mutual. The Dexters were labelled 'Eyeties'. Neither was the physical presence, for which Ted's sporting exploits became renowned, evident in his infancy. During the family's brief sojourn in Wales, Ted was sent to a prep school in Tenby. On his first morning, he found he simply wasn't strong enough to push open the school door, so he turned on his heel and walked home again.

The last of his prep schools was Norfolk House, near Beaconsfield in Buckinghamshire, only just up the A40 from Ealing, where he was to set up home and business on his retirement from cricket. Norfolk House has long since closed its classrooms – it became a home for disturbed girls – but it has the distinction of being the place where E. R. Dexter first showed an interest in cricket and a talent for batting. It was here, aged nine, that he made his first half-century.

Dexter had fallen on his cricketing feet at Norfolk House, where the headmaster, a Mr Glover, was extremely keen on the game and good enough at it to have played in the Minor Counties championship. Reflecting on this good fortune, Dexter said of Glover: 'He insisted that everything was done properly. I had a firm grounding in the basics. That was old Glover's way. He made sure that you got everything right at cricket from the very beginning.'

Already, however, the Dexter personality was making its mark. A prep school report chastized him thus: 'He shows promise at cricket but he must remember he still has much – in fact almost everything – to learn and is not yet in a position to control and give instructions to his fellows, who quite frankly resent it.' There are those who will say that this judgement on Dexter held good for many years after he emerged from the education system.

Norfolk House ceased operations during Dexter's last scheduled year there but instead of being a tiresome complication, entailing yet one more upheaval, it was a blessing. John was already installed at Radley and, through the family link, they agreed to take the younger brother a term early. Ted entered public school for the summer term of 1948, which meant that he enjoyed six cricket seasons at Radley rather than five. During the first of them, he made a century in a house match, an achievement sufficiently rare to identify him as a player of unusual potential.

The Radley of today is an enviable place in which to grow up. It was not quite so attractive immediately after the deprivations of wartime. One of Ted's peers described it as Dickensian. 'It was bleak, badly lit, poorly decorated and the rationed food in Hall, which regularly consisted of stewed whale meat, made it a somewhat daunting place to a new boy.'

If Dexter was at all daunted, he never betrayed it. No doubt it helped to have his elder brother there to show him the ropes and afford him a certain amount of protection from the rougher elements, but it helped, too, that both Dexters looked, and behaved, a cut above the average boy. They dressed with a style and elegance utterly beyond most boys in their early teens and both brothers appeared effortlessly adept at whatever they chose to turn their talents to. John, both then and later, was by all accounts the more personable and gregarious of the brothers and became immensely popular, but Ted's bearing and ability quickly ensured that he received a due degree of respect and admiration.

14

Michael Martin arrived at Radley on the same day as John and remained one of his closest friends for the rest of his life. But he also befriended the younger Dexter, still knows him intimately and is in a better position, perhaps, than anyone alive to assess the impact of the Dexter boys on this Oxfordshire public school. 'Despite the great difficulties of those post-war years,' recalls Martin, 'this was a golden age at Radley. We were brilliantly taught, both academically and on the playing-fields, but even great schoolmasters need to be cheered and inspired by outstanding boys. Both John and Ted were outstanding in every way. From the very start, they were different from the other lads. We were scruffy compared to the way the Dexters dressed and their cosmopolitan upbringing made them more mature than the rest of us. They always seemed older than their peers and, as they were both naturally athletic, they excelled at every game they played. John was not the sporting genius that Ted was, but he would have been considered very good if Ted had not been in the same school at the same time. Yet I was never aware of any great sense of rivalry between them. I always thought they got on exceptionally well.'

They must have had a certain style to convey such an impression, for Ted's recollection of brotherly relations is rather different. 'Like most brothers, our relationship was very much on a love–hate basis and to outsiders it must often have seemed that hate came out on top. We were forever scrapping about something and some of the fights may well have looked pretty realistic. Often, they felt realistic, too.'

This competition extended to sporting pursuits, in which John invariably came off second best to his kid brother. Although he made the school team at most games he played, and was considered a brave rugby full-back and a decent fast bowler, John never aspired to the heights that Ted inhabited as if by right. John was probably most proficient at golf, the one game to which he remained devoted all his life, but even here he suffered by comparison. Ted later recalled: 'As the years passed, golf became John's number one relaxation. Our matches were always fiercely

15

contested and I have to say I did not lose too many. Hardly surprisingly, that was anything but popular with big brother. Even much later, when we used to meet up on some Italian golf course two or three times a year, the result was generally just as it used to be during our schooldays. So lengthy, in fact, was my golfing domination of brother John that he said he developed a blank spot about playing me and was resigned to the fact that he would seldom win.'

The brothers' enthusiasm for golf, at a time when it had a far lower profile among the young than it does today, was inbred. Their father had always been a keen golfer and, on returning to Italy after the war, Ralph Dexter discovered that the Menaggio course, a short walk from the family's home beside Lake Como, had become disused and overgrown. In partnership with a Scotsman, Sir James Henderson, and a Swiss named Schmidt, Mr Dexter rebuilt and transformed the course. It was a painstaking job, and it was three years before all eighteen holes were once again playable, but the process was fascinating for the brothers when they visited in school holidays. Ted was just eleven when, with a borrowed club, he hit a golf ball at Menaggio for the first time and was bitten by the bug that still consumes him today. 'Golf began to dominate my holidays. Once in Menaggio, the game took me over. My father encouraged me, though he never pushed me to play. He was a fervently keen golfer himself, of average ability, and there were two features of his game which immediately rubbed off on me. The first was a natural hook and the second was his suspect temperament.

'Father's rages, when he fluffed a shot, were frequent and fierce and for some time I followed his example, perhaps thinking it was the thing to do. Later, probably when I reached that rebellious age when doing something differently from one's parents is infinitely preferable to being similar, I went entirely the other way. Temper and tantrums vanished from my game and, but for the very odd exception, never reappeared.'

Away from the golf course, temper was an emotion not associated with either Ted or his elder brother. At school, indeed, they

16

were considered model pupils. Douglas Birks, a master at Radley for thirty years, taught both Dexters and remembers them fondly. 'John was a wonderful chap, pretty quiet but with a genuine dignity about him, rare for his age. I taught him French and he eventually spoke it far better than I did. Ted was also fluent – good enough to play the lead in a Molière play the school put on – but my lasting impression is of his common sense. He was a serious-minded boy. Maybe he didn't have a lot of mental imagination but he had a very good brain and simply dealt with things as they arose. He didn't waste his time at school. You would never see him hanging around, kicking his heels and talking to his mates, as most boys would do. Nor would you see him laughing and joking very often. Perhaps he didn't have many really close friends, but I certainly don't recall him having a single enemy. Everyone admired Ted. Everyone was proud to know him.'

The most obvious reason for his popularity is that he was good at everything, though not in the sense of the scholarly swot who, in every generation, finds himself resented and rejected by his schoolmates. Ted was naturally gifted at those recreational pursuits which, down the years, have always decided the pecking order within a school. Those who pass every exam with honours will traditionally be thought too clever for their own good and regarded with great suspicion, but any boy who can score tries for the rugby team or run the 100 metres in school-record time will attain a celebrity status.

Ted Dexter was far from negligible where examinations were concerned but, among his peers, his intellect counted for nothing against his sporting prowess. Douglas Birks, himself a good enough cricketer to have played for his native Suffolk when they won the Minor Counties title in 1946, observed the phenomenon with keen interest. 'Radley was a very friendly school but it retained some Victorian ideas. The boys, who were all boarders, were not allowed to eat outdoors, for instance, and they had to seek permission if they wanted to go into Oxford, which is about three miles away. At that time, they also had to play a game every day of the week, and a Games Book was kept in which they signed their name against whatever they had played. There were always boys who tried to avoid games but Ted's problem was being spoiled for choice. Apart from rowing, which I don't recall him ever doing, he was outstanding at everything. 'In the Easter term, when the boys divided into "dry bobs" and "wet bobs", Ted played rackets and hockey. He was good enough at rackets to reach the final of the Public Schools doubles and, although he never took hockey very seriously, I can vividly remember a shot of his which hit the backboard harder than anything I had ever seen.'

The winter term meant rugby and Birks relates that, during Ted's two years as fly-half, the school lost only two matches. 'It was a case of "give it to Dexter". He had a great long stride and was so very strong.' This bears out the story of a visiting head-master who, having watched Dexter dominate an under-16 rugby match against his own school, remarked to his Radley counterpart that it was a quaint idea of his to take on boys *after* their National Service . . .

It was in the summer term, of course, that Ted really came into his own, not exclusively on the cricket ground. He was also a fine athlete and might have reached great heights but for the knee trouble which began late in his schooldays and has plagued him all his life. Not only could he run faster and jump further than the average boys, he demonstrated a remarkable versatility. One day, Douglas Birks showed an inquisitive Dexter the mechanics of the shot-putt. 'I told him how to hold the shot and he immedi-ately did 39 feet. Within a week, he was doing 45 and 46 feet, quite exceptional for anyone of that age, let alone a boy with such limited practice. When I demonstrated the discus to him, he was just as good. He could do everything and, although we had only one school athletics match each year, against Bradfield, Ted could have his choice of events.'

Michael Martin was another to marvel at Dexter's resourceful-ness and sums up his friend's dexterity with a simple example. 'Boys of our age have always improvised and imitated ball games.

For instance, we would throw up a stone and try to hit it with a cricket stump. I would manage it about once in every ten throws but Ted would hit the stone firmly every time.'

Another of Martin's reminiscences typifies this image of Dexter but also acts as a reminder that the Radley of the early 1950s was no tranquil paradise. 'It was in some ways a savage place in those days. Bullying was rife and an awful lot of beatings, with a cane, were handed out by both masters and senior pupils. For the weaker boys, this definitely cast a shadow over life, and although Ted was far from weak, I do clearly remember a day when he had been badly beaten by one of the seniors. I don't know what he had done wrong, if anything, but afterwards he came down to the school lake, which was much more my territory than his. I was secretary of the Radley trout fishing club, which shows that even the unathletic types could find their sporting niche there, and I could often be found at the lake of an afternoon. I remember being surprised to see Ted, and even more surprised when he asked me if I could show him how to cast a fly. Over the years, I have taught this to hundreds of people and it is an art which often takes them several weeks to master. Ted, who was no fisherman and had never even attempted it before, cast his fly perfectly within five minutes.

'Whether he was just trying to take his mind off the beating, I don't know, but I never saw him fish again at school. In fact, the only time since I have known him fish was when he caught a salmon in Scotland a few years back. He was so excited by this that he phoned me up and asked me if I would come round for dinner, first to help him carve it, which can be tricky, and then to eat it. I gladly turned up to his home in Ealing and, once carved, the salmon was put proudly on the sideboard while we had a pre-dinner drink. That was the last we saw of it. Our dinner was eaten by Ted's dog!'

There remains a depth and understanding in friendship between Dexter and Martin. In August 1993, in the week of Dexter's unhappy resignation as chairman of the England cricket committee, Martin phoned his old schoolmate to commiserate. Dexter was grateful, because precious few took the trouble to find out how he was feeling, and the two agreed to meet in London for dinner the following evening. Martin opened a bottle of champagne at his home in Chelsea, which was duly drunk before they moved on to a nearby restaurant he had booked – somewhere quiet and exclusive, he thought. Any prospect of avoiding the issues at hand vanished, however, when they were shown to their seats and there, at the next table, was a party of three including the new England captain, Michael Atherton.

The friendship was forged during their final two years at Radley, when the two of them, and a north-country boy named Kit Hood, shared a study. 'Ted was a far better scholar than either Kit or myself. I was pretty lackadaisical and larked about. I remember there was a school rule which said we must not have radios in our studies. I got around that by cutting the centre out of a big volume of Shakespeare and fitting a radio in the book. Kit was always up to something, too, but Ted was more serious about his work. He always tried very hard with his homework and, interestingly, he responded best to the teachers who were really hard taskmasters.'

Dexter was not, however, an outstanding scholar. He was plenty bright enough to pass exams, and ensured that he devoted sufficient time to the subject to do so, but as his schooldays came to their close, there were so many distractions. One of his last Radley reports contained the sardonic comment: 'In the intervals between cricket matches and A-level exams, he has written two adequate essays.' Not exactly a warm and glowing testimony.

Others in authority at Radley, though, regarded Dexter highly. Gradually, more and more responsibility was put his way. He was regularly asked to read the lesson in chapel and, with his strong, cultured voice, carried it off in style. While Michael Martin sang in school operas ('everyone could find their niche at Radley') Ted showed an unsuspected aptitude for the piano, and for drama. More predictably, given his physical size and reputation, he became senior in the Radley corps. His duties were to organize and supervise manoeuvres for the student troops on each Field

Day. For Ted, this role had a hidden bonus as the master in charge of the corps was Neil Fisher, an enthusiastic and above-average golfer who had always encouraged Dexter's interest in the game. More than once, when the teenage troops had been dispatched on some improvised mission, Fisher would suggest to Dexter that there was time for nine, or even eighteen holes, and the two of them would repair to the Frilford Heath club, eight miles from the school.

Fisher became more friend than schoolmaster to this imposing young man who had made such an impact on everyone at Radley. So much of an impact, in fact, that it was by unargued right that he was made Senior Prefect, or Head Boy, in his final year. The minor shocks and scandals which affect every boarding school, usually relating to illicit drinking or sex with either gender, had never tainted Dexter and, although he is remembered for his shy nature as much as his scholarliness and sporting genius, there is also a common recollection that he had no difficulty imposing discipline.

According to Douglas Birks: 'He could stand apart from the other prefects. He didn't need their support to decide what was right and wrong and to act upon it. One day during the performance of a school play, there was a bit of a disturbance at the back of the theatre. Ted became aware of this and took such exception that he used his authority as Senior Prefect and called the whole school together. There were about four hundred boys at Radley, then, but Ted was strong enough to give out a rollocking and to be respected for it.'

Sporting stardom, of course, would have helped Dexter carry this off, and sporting stardom he had in plenty. By this time, he was into his fourth successful season in the Radley cricket eleven. Naturally, he was captain. He had also, by the age of eighteen, played four times at Lord's where, ten years later, he was to play what many, though not Dexter himself, still believe to be his finest ever innings for England.

It was in the summer of 1950, when only just past his fifteenth birthday, that Dexter, E. R., joined Dexter, J. D., in the Radley side. He played fifteen times that season, averaging 31.90 with the bat and taking 26 wickets, having by then given up a dalliance with wicketkeeping that he took with him to Radley, and having begun to bowl at medium pace. Radley were unbeaten that year, though there was nothing unique about that. In the four seasons Dexter spent in the team, they were never once defeated by another school and suffered only two defeats against the nomadic adult clubs which customarily complete the fixture lists of public-school elevens.

This record owed much to the talent available, for apart from the Dexter brothers the side included Christopher Walton, later to play for Middlesex, and Clive Carr, a fine batsman who was to accompany Ted on National Service and then to Cambridge. But it also owed a good deal to the skill and enthusiasm with which cricket was then taught at Radley by men such as the professional Bert Robinson, who had plied his trade as a seam bowler for Northamptonshire, and by the master who had the greatest influence on Dexter's early cricket, Ivor Gilliat.

Dexter recalls Gilliat's gifts for imparting the psychology of sport. He also remembers him being 'a stickler for good manners', so that Radley teams, in the custom of the age, would 'receive' visiting school sides, carry their bags to the changing rooms and entertain them to meals during the game. Other masters of the time remember Gilliat as a brilliant eccentric, one who achieved success and popularity despite, or perhaps due to, his idiosyncrasies.

Today's politically correct society, in which teachers must conform to rigid, moralistic guidelines, would not have suited the Radley of the 1950s. In particular, it would have driven Ivor Gilliat to distraction and, almost certainly, unemployment, for he was a character who liked to teach in his own way, and if that indicated regular use of the cane on any errant fourth-former, he would carry that out as unhesitatingly as, in other circumstances, he would entertain the favoured boys to supper.

Gilliat was a man of private income, who taught at a public school because he enjoyed the lifestyle, more than through any

22

need of a salary. He was immensely well educated himself, of a background which bordered on upper class, and of leanings which paint him as Corinthian. He was a confirmed bachelor and an avid *bon viveur*. He was also, in the words of Michael Martin, 'enormously fat', though this did not prevent him staying active in the sports field. In his own youth, he had kept wicket for Oxford and played rackets to a decent level. As Radley's master in charge of cricket, he conducted regular and vigorous fielding practices, barking out commands and complaints in a voice that brooked no argument.

Gilliat was one of three masters who dominated the school during the Dexter brothers' years there. Another was Robin 'Tiny' Southam, who was social tutor, or housemaster, to John and Ted until his untimely death at the age of forty-two. The third was Theo Cox. The three were close friends as well as colleagues and, together, they moulded many a young life.

Certainly, Gilliat was responsible for the way in which Ted Dexter approached cricket. As he later recalled of his Radley days: 'I found that cricket there was seen as an essential part of one's education . . . nothing that sullied either the etiquette or the beauty of the game was tolerated at Radley.' This was the work of Gilliat, who, while devoting much time to explaining the mental processes involved in achieving superiority at cricket, would have heatedly condemned any tactic remotely dubious or underhand. He also instilled in his boys an awareness that cricket was to be enjoyed for its social possibilities as well as its more obvious sporting challenges. Each season, Radley played an away fixture at Eastbourne College, during which Gilliat would hold a dinner party in the plush restaurant of the Grand Hotel, where the boys would be treated to the sights and sounds of their master in his pomp, holding court on the issues of the day and bullying the waiters over any slackness with the wine list.

This is not to say that he took the cricket lightly. The school's record, during those heady days, should be sufficient proof of the priority given to a successful Radley side. Early in each season, net practice would be organized three afternoons a week, and there would often be at least two matches scheduled each week. For those of the younger Dexter's enthusiasm, Sundays provided further opportunity for practice. Ted explains: 'Most Sundays, I would be in the nets all day, apart from going twice to chapel. I practised incessantly, working at all departments of the game. Of course, it didn't seem like work at the time . . .'

Ted's second year in the eleven, 1951, was his least successful and provided one of the few instances of his brother upstaging him on a sporting field. Ted averaged only 29 with the bat, despite one score of 94, and his 26 wickets cost 18 runs apiece. Brother John was the team's strike bowler. It was his final term at Radley and he marked it by taking 54 wickets at 13 apiece, under the captaincy of Christopher Walton.

Among a number of promising cricketers then at the school, Ted might not have been considered outstanding. But in the summer of 1952, he began to play with a style and maturity given to precious few schoolboys. As Radley once more completed the summer unbeaten, Ted scored 581 runs at an imposing average of 83. His first school century came in that season. So, too, did selection for the Southern Schools team. Along with Walton, having his second year as Radley captain, Dexter played in the annual match at Lord's against The Rest and, by top scoring with 44, gained a place in the Public Schools side, representing all England, for the two-day game, again at Lord's, against Combined Services.

Dexter made 8 and 43 but he also made the acquaintance of two players in the opposition, both fresh out of school and into their National Service, who he came to know much better in succeeding years. Included in the Combined Services team were Sapper M. J. Stewart, later to be England's team manager when Dexter took over as chairman, and A/C F. J. Titmus, who was to become a team-mate at Test level and, eventually, an England selector and observer.

There were two other, unconnected, events during 1952 which were destined to have repercussions throughout Dexter's life. The first was that he sustained knee trouble. The second was that

Ivor Gilliat dubbed him 'Lord Edward'. The cartilage problem, doubtless, seemed no more than a passing irritant at the time but Dexter's knees have plagued him ever since and demanded many hours on the operating table. The nickname was adopted one Saturday evening when Dexter neglected his duties as secretary to the cricket team. One of his weekly tasks was to telephone the scores of the Saturday match through to the agency responsible for collating and releasing all school results. On this particular evening, Ted was dining with friends when he realized he had forgotten to make the call. As he did not have the day's scores to hand, he instead contacted the master, getting him out of his bath, and asked if he could phone them through instead. This said something about Dexter's relationship with Gilliat but rather more about the Dexter personality. Gilliat evidently thought so, anyway. More amused than annoyed, he mockingly referred to his pupil as 'Lord Edward', and the name stuck. It has been employed on countless occasions since then, not always with flattery in mind, and when the media campaign to oust him as England chairman was at its vitriolic peak, its use was sometimes plain offensive. At least during his playing days, however, the subject was happy with the label. 'I've enjoyed it,' he said. 'I have had a lot of fun out of it, and some thundering good publicity.'

There was, mockery aside, already a genuine touch of lordliness about Dexter's bearing. His ironic sense of humour set him apart from the juvenile japes of his peers as plainly as did his elegantly cut clothes. He was also unconsciously aloof in that nose-in-the-air style of one who may look as if he is being rude but, in Dexter's case, is merely so lost in thought that he neither sees nor recognizes those he is apparently blanking. He was already tending to mix with people older than himself, and to display an absolute contentment with his own company, rare in one so young. But it did not make him remote, or unpopular. Far from it. As his sporting deeds, specifically now on the cricket ground, attracted ever more attention, so he unwittingly won ever more admirers. And now, despite the bar on being seen with girls inside or outside the school grounds, they were not exclusively male admirers. Dexter was fast becoming a magnet for the pretty girls of Oxfordshire, without even needing to encourage the trend.

His appointment as cricket captain for his final year was a natural progression. It would not have seemed right for anyone else to do the job, for by now his cricketing prowess had assumed near legendary proportions. Example: it is said that Dexter played an on-drive, as he did with such proficiency throughout his career, against a visiting club side, and that it was struck with such power that it travelled all along the ground a distance of 270 yards. Who measured this feat is not clear, but the shot has been passed down the Radley grapevine with such certainty that it seems churlish to doubt it.

Another example: during a match against Eastbourne, Radley were running out of time to complete victory. Eastbourne were 140 for nine in the penultimate over and their number five batsman was unbeaten with 60 and anxious to retain the strike. He played the ball to fine leg and instantly settled for a single but Dexter, the captain, is said to have shouted for the fielder there to allow the ball to pass for four. This allowed Radley an over at the number 11 and provided an early instance of acute, innovative leadership.

Dexter, by all accounts, made a success of his time as captain, and not merely in terms of results. Douglas Birks was heavily involved in Radley cricket that summer and he recalls: 'He had a very good cricket brain and was always on the ball as captain. Perhaps it was because he was always a success that he maintained such a level of enthusiasm but I was certainly surprised to hear in later years how he would apparently wander off into the outfield when captaining a county side, or even England. At Radley, he was a very thoughtful captain. He knew how to handle his players and we were a very happy team, with no prima donnas. I never saw Ted lose his temper on the field. In fact, the only time I remember him getting upset was in a match against Stowe, and that was entirely impatience with himself. Stowe had rumbled him, setting a short mid-wicket for that back-foot force he always played so well. Ted insisted on playing the shot anyway, and was caught off it. He wasn't very happy.'

Birks could not recall if Ted's parents had been present on that occasion, but it would have been in keeping if they were. For some unaccountable reason, Dexter failures in school matches always seemed to coincide with the weekends when Ralph and Elise Dexter were over from Italy. This was not lost on either parents or son and as one of the big occasions of the 1953 season loomed, a two-day game against their enduring local rivals, Bradfield, Ted was blissfully unaware of any planned attendance by his mother and father. The senior Dexters, however, were determined to be present and the subterfuge was complex. Ralph Dexter was discovered by the headmaster of Bradfield in a cemetery adjoining the ground, peeping out from behind a tombstone, intent on remaining unseen by Ted. The covert operation was later deemed worthwhile. Radley won the match by an innings and 139 runs and the contribution of E. R. Dexter was a record in the hundred years of the fixture: with the bat, he scored 147 in only 110 minutes and, with the ball, he took seven for 46.

Dexter's bowling was to become an enigmatic part of his cricket. Many believed it was underrated and that he could, with the right commitment, have become that real rarity, a genuine fast-bowling all-rounder. But he was never committed to bowling and neither did his body, with its suspect knees, encourage him to over-exert. But at school, as much as later, he could be devastating when in the mood. In that final year, he took 47 wickets at 13.48 and Douglas Birks still vividly recalls a spell against a strong club side, Harlequins. 'We were being smashed around, which was quite unusual even against adult opposition, but Ted thought it was time to take a hand and decided to bowl quick. For the next few overs, he rushed in off 15 paces and bowled faster than anyone I ever saw in my years at Radley.'

These were isolated instances. Big innings from Dexter were commonplace. He was not far short of 1000 runs in school games that summer, again averaging 80, but he had a disappointment to come in the end-of-term games at Lord's. For the South against The Rest, he made 3 and 23; for the Public Schools against Combined Services, who now included his old friend and captain

27

Christopher Walton, he scored 2 and nought. The following year's *Wisden* commented that Dexter 'did not come off at Lord's. He suffered from impulsiveness and, time after time, got himself out before allowing himself a preliminary look at the ball.'

If this was cutting criticism, the caveat that followed would have heartened him. 'Not that anyone should censure him for being aggressive-minded. Dexter erred on the right side and it is to be hoped that as he learns discretion, there will be no sacrifice of those splendid scoring strokes.' There was none. But, as school-days ended and the Army beckoned, there were to be times when cricket might have been sacrificed altogether.

Chapter Two

Five years after leaving school, Ted Dexter was playing cricket for England. At the age of twenty-three this made him, by traditional English standards, an ambitiously young selection, yet he would assuredly have played sooner but for the intrusion of National Service. As it turned out, two years in the Army so demotivated Dexter towards cricket that he could conceivably have given up the game altogether.

During the 1950s a spell in the services no longer contained such transparent threat or promise, depending on one's attitude to war. For those not imbued with a passion to fight, beyond natural patriotism, this doubtless made National Service a less forbidding prospect. But perhaps for some, its revised military function, keeping the peace rather than winning a war, inevitably meant that the majority of the two-year stint was plain dull. Dexter confesses to being bored by his Army life. This, despite living the relatively comfortable peace-time existence of an officer and, through a lack of serious military activity, having ample spare time to indulge his various sporting interests.

He had no intention of making a career in the services. At that stage, indeed, he had no clear idea what might lie ahead in the way of gainful employment, aside from a vague assumption that the family insurance business, now thriving in Milan as never before, would have a job awaiting him if he wished to choose that course. Like most boys in their late teens and just out of school, Ted was intent on making the most of what freedom he had. There was life to be lived and girls to be enjoyed.

For a time, life accommodated him. While at Officer Cadet

School, he finished each day's duties by 6 p.m. and usually managed to be back in London an hour later ready for whatever social pleasures the night had in store. He was young, handsome, educated and wealthy. Few could have asked for more. Six months in Carlisle were not quite so pleasant. Ted was posted to the 57th Training Regiment of the Royal Armoured Corps and the care of the aptly named Corporal-of-Horse Bashforth. 'He was stern, tough and completely uncompromising,' recalled Dexter, 'but looking back from the safety of a few decades, I will concede that he knocked us into shape very efficiently. We all left his care very much fitter than when we had first set rather wary eyes on him.'

This regime did not entirely preclude a social life and the late nights in which the young Dexter indulged seem, occasionally, to have left him short of the prescribed level of military alertness. Against himself, indeed, he tells the story of one day dozing off when in charge of a convoy of armoured cars on Salisbury plain. As Dexter failed to respond to increasingly frantic wireless signals, the exercise was reduced to shambles.

The training complete, a posting to Malaya followed, as a second lieutenant in the 11th Hussars, Royal Armoured Corps, the unit known as the 'Cherry Pickers'. Now, it really was time to forsake the lights of London for a while, and it was a slightly wistful Dexter who took out his girlfriend of the moment for a farewell dinner. Here, too, however, his innate vagueness reared its head. He paid the restaurant bill by cheque but omitted to sign it. The cheque duly followed him all the way to Malaya.

And quite a journey that proved to be. The modern military would be flown to such a destination inside half a day, a swift and painless swap of one lifestyle, and one continent, for another. The 11th Hussars, *circa* 1954, were obliged to make four overnight stops during their tortuous flight in a York aircraft to their new base at Seramban, home to E. R. Dexter for the next eighteen months.

At the end of that time, Dexter's verdict on the experience was 'mostly unrewarding and boring'. Apart from the occasional venture into the jungle, when a close watch for ambushes was necessary, the routine was never dramatic and, to one of Dexter's sophisticated background, unfulfillingly mundane. Sporting diversions were welcomed at first but, come the end of his time, even those seem to have presented more a chore than an escape.

Rugby games were a regular feature, largely through the enthusiasm of the visiting Fijians. As one of few in the Hussars who had any rugby-playing experience, Ted remembers feeling 'something of a fall-guy. More times than I care to recall, Dexter was delegated to round up a side for a game with the visitors, only to find that they knew a great deal more about rugby than we did and would administer a beating by sixty or seventy points.'

Golf was also available: there was a small course close to the Seramban camp, but for one who had been smitten by the game in Menaggio, and played whenever possible at Radley, Ted was now strangely indifferent. 'In all the time we were there, I doubt if I used the course more than half a dozen times. My one abiding memory is of standing on the first tee, taking an enormous swing and missing the ball altogether – a misjudgement which could squarely be blamed on the quality of the regimental entertainment the previous evening.'

As to cricket, Dexter's record as a schoolboy prodigy had doubtless preceded him and he was hastily recruited to play for the Negri Sembilan state side. It was essentially the same game he had been playing at school, of course, but conditions could hardly have been more different. Instead of the true, trustworthy pitches at Radley which had nurtured his front-foot game, Dexter now encountered the rough matting pitches used around the East. And instead of the even, equable light of an English summer he had the harsh Malayan glare. 'I hardly made a run in my first season there,' he related ruefully.

By the next year, disillusionment had begun to take root. Whether most influenced by his surroundings, the people he was marooned with or the things he would rather have been doing, Dexter anticipated further fixtures for Negri Sembilan without enthusiasm. Indeed, in a letter to his parents back in Italy, he wrote: 'I'm afraid I am beginning to think life too short to spend days of it at a time playing cricket in the same unattractive place . . . cricket is all-powerful and lets nothing interrupt it.'

These were not the thoughts of one keen to aspire to the peaks of the game and, at the time, such was the last thing on Dexter's agenda. He knew, by then, that a place awaited him at Jesus College in Cambridge, where brother John was already resident, but he could see no attraction in playing cricket there. He would, in fact, have confined all sporting activity at Cambridge to the golf course but for the intervention of his father, on behalf of rugby, and of John for cricket.

He arrived in Cambridge in the autumn of 1955. He was there, ostensibly, to read Modern Languages, French and Italian, and he set out with no intention of idleness. Other things simply took him over, so that 'I was to distinguish myself by failing to attend one lecture all the time I was there.' Unsurprisingly, he emerged three years later with no degree to show for his sojourn, despite changing subjects midway through his course. 'As my work levels diminished, I had switched to English, thinking I had more chance of scraping through. But when it came to it, I sat the first couple of exams, realized it was a hopeless cause and didn't bother to turn up for the others.'

Dexter was not a wastrel by nature, and evidently was not short of the intelligence needed to scrape a pass mark, so we have to assume that his days and hours were otherwise filled. The social life on offer to well-heeled undergraduates of the 1950s accounted for some but, against his original intentions, sport took up an inordinate amount of his time, probably with an emphasis that would not be countenanced by the academic varsities of today.

John had balanced his time somewhat differently, hence his second in history and economics – not that he spent all his time studying, for it is doubtful that there was a more popular, personable or gregarious young man in college. Like his father and grandfather before him, he became a member of the Natives, a kind of avant-garde social club which devoted itself to the good things of life, like eating oysters and drinking fine wines. He also continued as a games player of above-average ability, playing cricket for

32

Jesus and, in his final year, captaining the university rugby team.

Perhaps it was this achievement of John's that persuaded Ralph Dexter that his younger son should play rugby, too. Whatever the motivation, he told Ted how much he disapproved of his notion to play nothing but golf in his freshman year at Jesus. 'This was unusual,' recalled Ted, later. 'Dad very seldom interfered in the lives of my brother or myself, preferring to let us make our own decisions and then help us to achieve our goals, but on this occasion he told me that he would be disappointed if I didn't play at least a little rugby. As he was paying the bills, I thought the request could scarcely be ignored, so for the first term I complied.' Although he had been thought outstanding at Radley, however, where he got by on his physical advantage over the rest of his age-group, Ted and rugby were not made for each other. 'I did not particularly care for the game and I would even admit now that I was probably a little soft for it.' It was not softness, though, that retarded any early advances he might have made but a freakish injury suffered at the very outset of his college's first rugby practice in October 1956. 'I was only just jogging onto the field when a ball bounced towards me and I casually hoofed it back. But in doing so, I experienced an unpleasant twanging feeling. I had torn my right hamstring but, having no conception of how to treat injuries, I attempted to play on, which naturally only made things worse.' He recovered sufficiently to play a few games for the Sixty Club, the Cambridge 2nd XV, and even played in the second-string university match against Oxford Greyhounds. 'Because we had so many top-class stand-off halves I had to vacate my normal position and play on the wing. We were soundly thrashed.' But further injuries frustrated him and he was not enjoying the game anyway. So, as 1957 dawned, he had his way, and took to the golf course.

The commonly held memory of Dexter the student is simply that he was a singularly high-class cricketer. And so he was. But while his deeds at Fenner's and farther-flung cricket grounds were creating around him the aura of fame waiting to happen, he was

33

also causing quite a stir at golf and enjoying that at least as much as his cricket.

Sport placed such demands on him that, eventually, he had time for nothing else. Well, nothing bar a decent social life, into which he threw himself with some gusto. Dexter had passed his driving test and, having set out on the road with an open-top Austin A40, he was soon behind the wheel of something far more stylish, a Rover 90 bought for him by his father. This was a greatly envied and heavily employed status symbol, at least until a night of revelries ended when he hit a bollard in Jesus Lane and bounced the prized Rover from one side of the road to the other.

Exceptional sportsmen are always popular among their peers but Dexter's eminence in the games department led to another perk. As his profile at the university rose, he became secretary of golf and cricket in 1957, his second year, and captain of both in his third. It was clearly necessary in such positions that he should be accessible, so instead of having to find his own living accommodation, as must most students after their freshman year, he was allowed to keep the same college rooms throughout his time at Jesus.

The Cambridge golf captain in 1956 was David Marsh, who subsequently led Great Britain's Walker Cup team and played a crucial role in the victory at St Andrews in 1971, only Britain's second in the event's history. Marsh was aware that Dexter was already a low-handicap player and took a keen interest when he gave up rugby for the Easter term of that first year. By then, however, the Cambridge team was pretty much settled and although Marsh played with Dexter more than once in the weeks leading up to selection for the Varsity Match, he missed out. Instead, Dexter was named as one of the travelling reserves who play what is known as the 'dinner match' on the day prior to the match itself, the losers having to pay for the following night's entertainment. 'I rather set the cat among the pigeons by playing the first nine holes of the tough Formby course in 32 – better than anyone else could manage the following day,' Dexter related.

It might have been a fleeting disappointment to him that he was given a role only in the warm-up act rather than the main event. But nothing more than that. 'Strange as it may seem, I was not at all ambitious in games at that stage. I was keen and competitive but, to me, they were just a bit of fun. I had been stuck away in Malaya for eighteen months and my idea of enjoying myself was to take girls out on the river. Sport became a more serious business for me when I was elected secretary of both the golf and cricket clubs the following year. This position is normally seen as a stepping-stone to the captaincy and is certainly an acknowledge-ment of the recipient's ability and a virtual confirmation that he will be in the side. The die was cast, and I responded.'

University golf matches usually took place at weekends and, often, the team would play at one club on the Saturday and another on the Sunday. It involved 36 holes each day, frequently on courses completely new to the students. But they were treated royally by most of the opposition clubs and the Saturday-night parties usually took them well into the Sabbath. There was a lot of travelling to be done, but closer to home lay the Royal Worling-ton club, twenty miles out of Cambridge and the closest thing the Cambridge team claimed to a 'home' course. Dexter recalls: 'It was a friendly club, whose members numbered a good deal of Newmarket racehorse trainers, not to mention that great cricketer-golfer and journalist, the late Leonard Crawley.' Worlington, indeed, had more influence on Dexter than he could possibly have realized at the time. By mixing with the racing crowd, his interest in horses, and gambling, began to grow. And by mixing with Leonard Crawley, a noted expert on the technical side of games, Dexter developed the passion for theory that is still so evident in him. 'Leonard loved discussing the theory of the golf swing, or of the batsman's grip, and much of this must have rubbed off on me, for in later life I find that these very same technical points fascinate me just as much as they did him.'

Ted loved Worlington as much for its regular patrons and its estimable food and drink as for the golf itself. 'In the clubhouse, a couple called Mr and Mrs Leader laid on far better lunches and teas than could be had anywhere else in the vicinity – an important consideration for hungry students.' But, while he enjoyed the social side of golf, he was also becoming a considerable player, as witnessed by his performance in the 1957 University Match. The venue was Royal St George's in Sandwich, Kent, distinguished by various Open Championships and as the home club of the veteran heavyweight cricket writer, E. W. Swanton. Dexter was drawn against one of Oxford's best, name of Foster, and at lunch, after 18 holes, he was three down. 'The afternoon round was one of the most inspired I ever played. I broke par four times and won on the 17th green. It was a success of which people were bound to take note as the university match was still of prime interest to amateur international selectors, and later that year I received the circular from the Walker Cup selectors informing me of the events at which they would be present the following season. This was accepted as meaning I was on the short-list.'

Dexter never did find out whether he could have made the Walker Cup team against the United States. Cricket dates coincided with golf and cricket was judged the winner. With that decision, he consigned golf to the social side of his life and promoted cricket above it. It was a pivotal verdict and, most would assume, the right one, but in years to come Dexter frequently wondered how good a golfer he might have become if he had decided differently.

At university, those who played golf were privileged beings, not only having their weekend social life organized for them but, at the end of the season, setting off on a tour. It was the job of the secretary to make the arrangements and, in Dexter's year, it was a predictably ambitious affair. 'We had been on a trip to Scotland, playing all the major courses, and then set off for the continent, playing through Spain, Switzerland and Italy. These trips were financed by the individuals, without college subsidies, but we managed to do it all very cheaply. Four men shared each car and we often just slept where we could.'

Just as often, though, the touring students were put up in fine hotels, none finer than in northern Italy, near the Dexter family home, where the team stayed at the palatial Villa d'Este Hotel on

Lake Como for a pound per head. 'The only condition was that we all played in the Italian Amateur tournament, staged on the hotel's course. It seemed a small price to pay for such luxury.'

With Dexter as captain, the Cambridge team engaged the services of John Jacobs, later to become Ryder Cup captain, to help them prepare for the 1958 Varsity golf match. It was to be held at Rye, Dexter's nomination as the choice fell to Cambridge on the alternate basis, and Jacobs went down to Sussex on one of the practice days. He showed the Cambridge players films of the top American golfers using a new theory, which involved standing left of target on the tee and firing the ball to the right. Dexter, now a slave to the technical side of the game and a devotee of the Ben Hogan book, *Modern Fundamentals of Golf*, absorbed this idea and eagerly put it to the test. 'I tried it on the practice ground and it worked reasonably well, but in competition it became a nightmare which was to stay with me for some time to come.'

Here, then, was an early example of Dexter blinding himself with science, one that he later freely conceded. 'The average golfer cannot possibly absorb such detail into his game and, in general, the more he thinks about theory, the worse he will become. That, certainly, was the way with me.' But he would also concede that this realization did not stop him pursuing and promoting any technical trivia which came his way.

Rye in 1958, however, holds happy memories for Ted. Oxford were duly beaten and Dexter won his own match, followed around the course in 'appalling, freezing weather' by his loyal girlfriend. 'She must have come close to abandoning our relationship on the spot,' he said. 'Fortunately she didn't, and she is now my wife.'

Ted had met Susan Longfield, the daughter of a Calcutta businessman, at a party, and was so taken by her that he overlooked etiquette in that she was then the girlfriend of his host. Tenacious in the hunt, he wrote letters both to Susan and her erstwhile boyfriend, seeking the company of the former and pleading the forgiveness of the latter. Somehow, he got away with the prize of the girl and the reluctant blessing of his party host, and so began a relationship often seen as glamorous – for Susan's beauty was a byword – which has endured through all manner of trials and remains the happiest partnership of Ted's life.

Back at Cambridge, most of Ted's friendships were formed on the golf course – which is, to some degree, still so today – but brother John, unbeknown to Ted, had entered his name on the list for freshmen's nets. 'I was already brooding about examinations,' he recalls. 'I reckoned that any spare time might be spent playing golf. I certainly had no intention of playing cricket. But John would not hear of me wasting my cricket ability and, despite my protestations, he pointed out that I was now bound to turn up for nets. That was really how my cricket career began, for in cricket, if you get selected, you play, and I kept being selected. From the freshmen's nets I graduated to the top twenty nets and from there to the freshmen's trials. I made runs, and suddenly found myself in the side for the first three university matches of the 1956 season.'

This had not been the Dexter plan but, as has happened at intervals throughout his life, events swept him along at an irresistible pace. He remembers those early nets as light-hearted affairs, certainly on his part, in which he simply batted for the fun of it. He also remembers being bowled out, time and again, by a seam bowler named Wheatley – the same Ossie Wheatley who, many years later, became chairman of the Test and County Cricket Board's cricket committee, with far-reaching effect, when Ted took on the chairmanship of the England committee.

Dexter and Wheatley were to become the outstanding Cambridge players of their day, though this was by no means obvious from the way Ted began his first-class career. The season opened against Surrey, which could hardly have been more daunting as they were in the middle of an uninterrupted seven years as county champions. Moreover, they fielded a representative team for the match at Fenner's and Dexter's first entry in the Cambridge scorebook was undistinguished: bowled Loader 0. 'It was a yorker which hit the stumps while my bat was still coming down,' he admits. 'In the second innings, Jim Laker bowled a long hop deliberately to give me one off the mark.' The gift gratefully accepted, Dexter went on to score 44 and begin to justify the lofty reputation that, like it or not, he had brought into the university side.

Bizarrely, Dexter made a nought in each of his first four games. They were failures of great significance because, far from discouraging him in this cricketing venture which had been pressed upon him, they so frustrated him that he set about discovering what he was doing wrong. Soon, the theory of batsmanship was fascinating him every bit as much as the theory of the golf swing. 'I went into those early games with a flourish. I just wanted to hit the ball hard and enjoy myself. But before long I was to spend hour after hour practising.'

This memory is endorsed by Ossie Wheatley, who recalls: 'Ted was the most hard-working undergraduate cricketer at Cambridge. He spent an enormous amount of time in the nets and was deeply interested in the technical side of the game. That was what motivated him and was one of the reasons why he was such a good player. Whenever he was out in a game, he'd be off to the nets, analysing how it happened and what he could do about it. He prepared himself for cricket very thoroughly. He has this Corinthian image but that does not relate to hard work, and Ted was a worker. I always thought he was lucky to have Cyril Coote, who spent a lot of time with him, helping with minor changes to his technique.'

Cyril Coote was, ostensibly, only the Cambridge groundsman, but to several generations of student cricketers he was a great deal more than that. An enthusiast for the game, talented enough to have reached Minor Counties standard himself, Coote struck up a rapport with Dexter, who now says: 'He taught me more about the wrinkles of the professional game than anyone else. He used to come out for hours, throwing balls just short of a length outside the off stump for me to try and crack off the back foot. And he warned me not to play the pull shot at Fenner's, because the bounce is too low, but always to play straight.'

Sound, fundamental advice like this was essential nourishment for Dexter's growing appetite for the game and it was to Coote that he increasingly turned for help. Not that too much help would have been thought necessary. Despite the grim start, and although county teams were already gunning for this young upstart who thought he could play shots against them, Dexter averaged 32 in that first summer of university cricket, and made two centuries. One was against Middlesex but the first, and most significant, was against Sussex.

At that time, Sussex were captained by Robin Marlar, who became the long-serving cricket correspondent of the *Sunday Times*, in which capacity he was a trenchant critic of Dexter's England committee. In 1956, however, Marlar was nearing the end of a playing career which had brought him almost 1000 wickets as an off-spin bowler and almost, though never quite, won him selection for MCC tours. 'After I had missed out on a couple of tours, I went to the West Indies with a side raised by Jim Swanton, early in '56, and it was then, bowling to the likes of Conrad Hunte and Rohan Kanhai, that I realized I was no good,' says Marlar, self-effacingly. 'I was an amateur throughout my cricket career and I worked as librarian for the Duke of Norfolk, but journalism beckoned and, by the end of that West Indies trip, I had an eye open for my successor at Sussex.'

Enter Dexter. The first impression he made on Marlar was to hit him for such an enormous, straight six that the ball had still not pitched when it struck the wall, 30 feet beyond the playing area at Fenner's. This, perhaps understandably, is not the memory Marlar volunteers from that game. 'For some extraordinary reason, I was fielding at cover when Dexter hit one off the back foot. I was like a statue as it went past me to the boundary, and that was enough to convince me. That evening, I began talking to Ted, pointing out that Brighton was about as near as he would get to Milan if he wanted to play county cricket.'

Dexter was not about to be rushed into anything, for he was not convinced he wanted to play county cricket. At that time, he was also doing what came increasingly unnaturally to him at Jesus College and swotting hard for exams. 'I was playing cricket almost every day but I used to get up early, study from seven until ten, play all day and then return to my rooms for another three hours' work. It was enough to get me through, and as there were no further university exams until the end of the third year, I knew I was fairly safe from being slung out.'

And then there was the Varsity Match to think about, the first of three that Dexter was to play in. This one was drawn, his contributions being 46 and 17, but the occasion was spoiled for him on the first morning of the game, when a letter was delivered to him by hand in the Cambridge dressing room at Lord's. His girlfriend of the previous four years, the one who had survived him saying farewell with unsigned cheques and being away in Malaya for eighteen months, was telling him it was over, and choosing a somewhat unkind moment for the bombshell. 'I felt pretty hard done by,' said Dexter. 'I never could understand why she didn't wait until the match was over.'

On the bounce from this relationship, he set off for Cambridge's end-of-term tour to Denmark, having promised Marlar that he would return to play a few games for Sussex towards the end of the season. It was a promise he was destined to break, and romance, or the prospect of it, was once more to blame. 'I was fascinated by an adorable girl in Copenhagen, so I stayed on and sent a postcard to Sussex saying I was sorry I could not play for them as arranged. At the time I thought it quite normal behaviour. When I look back on it now, I cringe.'

Those familiar with the temper of R. Marlar will be expecting to hear that he did something more voluble than cringe, probably followed by calling off the deal forthwith. This is not the case. 'Some of the Sussex committee were very jumpy about it and there was plenty of muttering about cavalier behaviour,' explains Marlar, 'but for once, I was less agitated, and told the committee members that this was a prize worth waiting for.'

So wait they did, and not without anxiety, for Dexter was now considered such a catch that many other counties were expressing interest. Perhaps partly shamed by the Copenhagen affair, but also because he liked what he had seen of Brighton and Hove, Dexter

41

was mentally committed to joining Sussex, although he had set no definite timetable. Still in his mind was the knotty problem of obtaining a degree; there were also two further summers of university cricket to be played, in the second of which he seemed sure to be Cambridge captain. Before much of this could proceed, however, life once again picked up Dexter and hurled him onwards as if he had landed on a ladder on a Snakes-and-Ladders board. For in the summer of 1957, the year in which *Wisden* described him as 'a stylist without parallel at either university', the England selectors voiced their agreement.

Dexter's first call to international arms followed a half-season in which his form was irrepressibly good. So good, in fact, that he was involved in a close-run race with Tom Graveney and Peter May for the honour of being first in England to reach 1000 runs. He made 185 against Lancashire, for whom Cyril Washbrook, fielding at cover, echoed the sentiments of Robin Marlar twelve months previously, saying he had never known a ball hit harder past him. Partly on the strength of this innings, he was then invited to play in a Centenary Match at Old Trafford, representing MCC against Lancashire. This was a stroke of luck for Dexter in more ways than one, for the game coincided with the dates of the college examinations, for which he had done not a stroke of work. His tutor, wise man, decided he should miss the exams and play in the match.

Washbrook was once more in the opposition and, once more, was impressed. Dexter made a half-century in the second innings and has not forgotten it. 'My recollection of the game is of one shot that I played . . . I hit it off the back foot through the covers and it was perfect. Cyril Washbrook reached down a hand to stop the ball and then realized that it was travelling at about 95 miles an hour and took his hand away with alacrity. Len Hutton, who was *the* great name in those days, came in and said to me, "Keep it up, lad." And I was out a couple of balls later.'

Robin Marlar also played in that match but his memory of it concerns Dexter's bowling. 'He took five wickets with big, devilish outswingers, swinging very late, and he showed he could also bring the ball back off the seam. I saw then that he had a fantastic, natural ability to bowl. With two extra yards of pace he could have taken on the world.'

It was, all things considered, a game that put Dexter on the map, perhaps more than any he had previously played. And the selectors were not slow to respond. Trevor Bailey reported unfit for the fourth Test against West Indies at Headingley and, to great public acclaim, the call went out for Dexter. Sadly, it was answered in the negative. Dexter, now registered with Sussex and being promoted for all he was worth by Marlar, had been brought on to bowl in a championship match against Northants and turned his ankle. England, like Sussex before them, were made to wait for him.

Chapter Three

As the 1950s ended, Ted Dexter was undoubtedly the envy of many men in Britain. Dashingly handsome and perceived to be tolerably rich, he was an England cricketer and a considerable golfer, a man with aristocratic style and a stunningly lovely wife. To the layman observer, the Dexter horizons were blue and cloudless – yet he was unfulfilled, insecure and subject to bouts of depression. During the autumn months of 1959, he also suffered the onset of two unconnected diseases – jaundice and gambling – which only served to darken his mood still further. Glamour is frequently confused with contentment and Ted was glamour personified. Contentment was something else. Cambridge had given him a public image as a shooting star but it had not given him qualifications. It had made him a justifiably famous sportsman, at a very young age, but it had not given him a degree. To an extent, this forced his hand over the future. Sport had claimed him for its own and, although golf remained a passionate love of his life, cricket was the obvious course to take, for his credentials were copper-bottomed and prospective employers needed to form a queue.

Dexter, however, never intended to play sport for money. Didn't need to, didn't want to. He was to be the last amateur registered for Sussex and one of the last to play for England. He played in the last Gentlemen's side, before the abolition of the annual match against the Players, or professionals, and in many ways he was the embodiment of the Corinthian profile. But, although money has seldom been his motivation in anything, the image of the idle dilettante does not sit comfortably on Dexter.

Then, as later, he wanted to occupy his mind and do something both practical and worthwhile with his life. It was in this, during 1959, that he felt frustrated.

There was no warning of this as Dexer completed university life, generally in flourishing good spirits that showed a bullish disregard for his academic failings. In the summer of 1957, when his tutor had allowed him to miss exams to play at Old Trafford and when the England selectors had thought enough of him to invite him to play in the Headingley Test, he also played a part – though an unusually insignificant one – in a notable Varsity Match at Lord's.

Cambridge had a considerable team that year and that they did not depend exclusively upon Dexter was amply demonstrated as they swamped Oxford by an innings and 186 runs, the biggest winning margin for either side since the Varsity Match was first played 130 years earlier. Dexter's contribution was a mere 7 out of the Cambridge total of 424 for seven declared and, as Oxford were bowled out for a humiliating 92 and 146, the first-innings damage was done by figures of five for 15 for Ossie Wheatley.

Dexter had a lot of time for Wheatley's bowling, and not only due to the regularity with which he had once bowled him out in the nets. The following summer, when Dexter took on the university captaincy, Wheatley was his prime fast bowler and responded by taking 80 wickets at 17.63, the best seasonal figures ever recorded by a Cambridge bowler. Wheatley was suitably grateful. 'I thought he was a good captain because he bowled me a lot,' he jokes now. 'We were not close friends, partly because we were not in the same college and partly because Ted's cronies tended to come more from the golf set. But I liked him well enough and, like everyone else at Cambridge at the time, respected his ability. As a captain he was never a great communicator. He was very modest, to the point of being self-effacing, and undoubtedly shy. His shyness used to be misinterpreted by many, who thought it a type of arrogance, but in fact, it was just that if Ted had nothing to say on a subject he would keep his head down. The irony to me is that he ended up in public relations, for he really wasn't suited to it.'

What he did best, of course, was score runs and, to the gratification of Robin Marlar down at Hove, take wickets. During the 1958 university programme, Dexter took 36 wickets, second only to Wheatley, but much his most significant spell of bowling came in the closing stages of his third Varsity Match, a much closer affair than his second but with the same outcome.

Chasing the game, after time had been lost to rain, Dexter made two declarations. He called off Cambridge's first innings at 161 for seven, which Oxford surpassed by 19 before being bowled out, then declared again at 269 for eight, making 58 himself. With time short to force a result, Dexter opened the bowling, giving another justification of the theory, espoused by many, that he would only bowl effectively when it most mattered. His first four overs brought three wickets for 3, leaving the Oxford innings in ruins at 11 for four, and although he strained a thigh in the process and was forced to take a rest, he brought himself back to shift a stubborn ninth-wicket pair and, inevitably, did so. Dexter finished with four for 14 and Oxford were beaten by 99 runs with six minutes to spare.

This was a typically dramatic end to Dexter's Cambridge career, though by then he was regarded as much more than a mere university cricketer. Out of term, he was making runs prolifically for Sussex, and the England selectors, stymied in their ambitious call for him the previous year, were about to issue a second and successful summons for his services.

The Test series that summer was against New Zealand but the selectors and cricket-watching public were already preoccupied by the Ashes tour to follow. Travel to Australia was still by ship in those days and the itinerary of the tour entailed departing soon after the end of the domestic season. To give the players – both the lucky and unlucky ones – enough time to make the necessary plans, it was arranged that the selectors should name the seventeen-strong party during the fourth Test with New Zealand in late July.

46

Dexter had an obvious chance. He had played consistently well for Cambridge against the counties that summer, scoring 1256 runs, including three centuries, at an average of almost 42. He had also done well in his second Gents versus Players game. And then there were the exciting, last-ditch heroics in the Varsity Match, a game that still commanded considerable publicity in the late 1950s. If selection for Australia had been handed over to the public, he would have been an automatic inclusion in the same way, ironically, as Ian Botham and David Gower would have been when Dexter's selection panel excluded them from touring, thirty years and more later. The 1958 selectors, however, first wanted to see how Dexter coped with a home Test match, so he was duly announced in the England side for the Old Trafford game against New Zealand.

It was Dexter's misfortune that Manchester's grim reputation for poor weather was upheld that week. When the game began, he thought with justification that he must have a good chance of inclusion in the touring party for, apart from Tom Graveney, Colin Cowdrey and the then captain, Peter May, the middle-order batting places were unclaimed. Dexter's chance to play had arisen through another injury to Trevor Bailey and he was scheduled to bat at number six. Two other players were making their Test début in the game: Raman Subba Row, later to chair the Test and County Cricket Board, and Ray Illingworth, who not only went on to captain England after Dexter's retirement but, in 1994, succeeded him as chairman of the England selectors. What coincidence!

Back in 1958, such high office was not even a long-range ambition, for the thoughts of all concerned were focused on producing a sufficiently strong personal performance to earn a berth on that ship bound for Fremantle. On the face of it, there could hardly have been a more comfortable opportunity. New Zealand had still never won a Test match against England and were particularly weak that summer. They had lost the first Test by 205 runs, their batsmen unable to handle the speed of Fred Trueman, and the next two by an innings, with the spin pairing of Tony Lock

47

and Jim Laker doing virtually all the damage. They came to Manchester a crestfallen, clearly outclassed team, with even their captain, the estimable John Reid, hopelessly short of runs. England had no Bailey, Cowdrey or Laker but nobody seriously believed it would matter.

Nor did it. England triumphed by an innings once again, becoming the first side in an English series ever to win the first four Tests. New Zealand, whose nadir had come in being dismissed for 47 and 74 on a rain-affected pitch at Lord's, again found Lock unplayable after bad weather. He took seven for 35 as a previously competitive game ended tamely in an all-out score of 85 on the final day. By then, however, the most newsworthy business of the five days had been conducted and Dexter knew that he was not among those chosen to go to Australia. It was all the fault of the weather. The selectors were due to pronounce on the Sunday, then sacred as a Test match rest day, and it was obviously anticipated that everyone would have had some chance to press a claim during the first three days. This, however, was reckoning without the traditions of Manchester. On the second evening, England closed at 192 for two, Graveney and May batting together and Dexter ready to put on his pads. It seemed his chance would inevitably come on the Saturday but, instead, only a few minutes' play were possible, in which Graveney was out. Dexter still sat, padded up and frustrated, in the Old Trafford pavilion.

He had no immediate cause to be down-hearted. For one thing, he had the irrepressible Godfrey Evans, England's wicketkeeper, for company as he headed out for a round of golf at the Mere Country Club the following day. A decent lunch, followed by a decent round, put Dexter in good spirits as the day developed. 'I clearly recall sitting with Godfrey in his Bentley, in the golf club car park, waiting for the six o'clock news on the radio to tell us the side. "Godders", in his usual manner, loudly swept aside all my doubts and spoke convincingly of why I would be chosen – but I wasn't.'

The following morning, Dexter finally got to the wicket and

scored 52 in a stand of 82 with May. 'The newspapers talked of a grave blunder that had been made in omitting me,' he recalled. But it was too late. Or so, at the time, it seemed. Selectors do not reverse decisions under public or media pressure, no matter how charismatic the personality involved, and Dexter himself was to demonstrate this in the 1990s, with David Gower the rejected player. Indeed, while there seemed little room to doubt that he would in time be a regular member of the side, Dexter's early treatment by those who hire and fire could be thought cavalier. It is acknowledged, these days, that a young player brought into the Test side should be given at least two games to make a mark. Dexter, having made 52 on début, was left out of the next match. Cowdrey, Bailey and Laker were all fit again and England, seeking a whitewash, put out what was considered their strongest side. In the event, more rain ruined the prospect of 5–0; two days were washed out and New Zealand gratefully took their leave with a respectable draw.

It was widely assumed that the final batting place for the Australian tour had gone to Subba Row, ahead of Dexter, and that it constituted a serious misjudgement. Subsequent years were to prove this assumption correct, for Subba Row had only a brief Test career, albeit including the rare distinction of centuries in his first and last games against Australia. Neither occurred on the tour in question, however, because Subba Row was one of several England players to be injured. Ironically, given the outcry over the original selection, it was when he was incapacitated with the broken bone in his hand that the SOS went out for Dexter to join the party.

Nowadays, this is a common and straightforward operation. Each tour undertaken by England has its standby players, who are paid a retaining fee to keep themselves fit, in reasonable practice and readily available to fly out at short notice. Modern air timetables add to the simplicity of the system. Airline schedules were not quite so accommodating in 1958 and, in the case of E. R. Dexter, there were additional complications. First, he had to be found.

49

Now that his education was over, Dexter reached the end of the 1958 cricket season with no clear idea of what the winter held in store for him. He was twenty-three and, to all intents and purposes, an out-of-work cricketer. With no great enthusiasm, he accepted the convenience of a temporary post in his father's insurance business, though not for the family company in Italy but for a family friend in Paris. The company was H. R. Sprinks and Ted's duties were neither strictly defined nor definitely restrictive. 'The life,' he concedes, 'was more social than business.'

By now, his romance with Susan Longfield had become an unstoppable whirlwind. He proposed marriage in the early part of that winter, and was accepted, but it was not until the summons to Australia arrived, during December, that the couple felt the need or inclination to announce their plans. After that, things began to happen rather fast.

Out in Australia, Peter May's side was in trouble. It had the look of a powerful team, certainly by today's standards, with May, Graveney and Cowdrey a classical middle-order, Bailey the ideal all-rounder at number six, wicketkeeper Evans at seven and, as the four specialist bowlers, Brian Statham, Peter Loader, Jim Laker and Tony Lock. Many recent England captains would have happily swapped places with May, yet the first Test in Brisbane had been lost heavily. It was a low-scoring and slow-scoring affair, quite the worst sort of game to be the first televised Test in Australia. Never did Bailey earn his 'Barnacle' nickname more thoroughly than here, in an innings of 68 which lasted almost eight hours. It was all in vain and Australia, required to score 147 in the fourth innings on the final day, were seen home by a third-wicket stand of 89, of which Norman O'Neill made an unbeaten 71. At the other end was Burke, every bit as intransigent as Bailey in his score of 28 not out, spanning 250 minutes.

This was a poor start to the series and, for England, things soon went downhill. Willie Watson, Arthur Milton and Bailey all suffered injuries and John Mortimore was called out as an additional spin bowler. It was when Subba Row's broken hand was diagnosed that May and his management team agreed upon

Dexter's recruitment. And so the fun began. Captaining Australia for the first time in that series was Richie Benaud, at twenty-eight already a highly respected figure whose analytical mind in years to come had a forceful bearing on the direction of Australian cricket. He still remembers hearing of the call for Dexter and of his team's reaction to it. 'If my memory is right, Ted was skiing in the Austrian alps when the call came that he was required in Australia. At the time, at our team meeting, we were of the opinion that it would be very difficult for him to arrive in Australia and make any kind of impact with the bat. Some of us knew of him, and what he had already achieved, but we did not know him as a person.'

They made his acquaintance soon enough, and formed some strong views, but in the meantime Dexter had to begin the most tortuous journey of his life. Before leaving Paris, he announced that he and Susan were engaged. To the media, already expending acres of newsprint on the story, this added to the fascination of the affair. 'The whole business of a newly engaged Cambridge man socializing in Paris and being flown to "save" his country in Australia captivated the journalists,' said Dexter. 'It had the splendour of an Edwardian romance.'

For Dexter, the splendour ended there. With no kit and no money to speak of, he first set his sights towards London, where both were being organized for him by MCC. His first flight was from Le Bourget airport outside Paris but the airfield was fog-bound and passengers were diverted to Orly. From there, he took off satisfactorily but London was in the grip of a real pea-souper and the pilot was unable to land. Some hours later, Dexter found himself back on the ground at Orly, chafing increasingly. At the second time of trying the plane managed to land at Heathrow, where Dexter was met by the secretary of MCC, 'Billy' Griffith. By now, though, he was not only tired but ill. A virus had attacked him, he ached all over and had lost his voice. And the incredible journey had hardly begun.

London to Sydney, *circa* 1958, was theoretically a two–day trip by air. It took Dexter five days, including a seventeen–hour delay for technical trouble in Bahrain. With the throat infection still troubling him, and understandably drained by the journey, he was in no condition to play cricket immediately and, for his first few days in Australia, he was looked after by a former English county player named John Human, who had settled in Sydney. Human, by all accounts, put up with a lot. Dexter was in a poor state, mentally and physically, and his host received few of the traditional courtesies. 'John later told me I really wasn't a likeable fellow in those few days,' recalled Dexter. 'He said I was off-hand, moody and ungrateful. It sounds awful and probably was.'

Eventually, he was fit enough to play and he took part in first-class games in Tasmania and South Australia before being named as twelfth man for the second Test in Melbourne which, on that tour, began on New Year's Eve rather than the now customary Boxing Day.

For England, this was a match which began badly and grew steadily worse. They were 7 for three after May had chosen to bat, the great left-armer Alan Davidson taking all three wickets in his second over of the match, and although a century from May restored order, they trailed by 49 on the first innings and were then dismissed for 87. It was England's lowest total in Australia for fifty-five years and brought about inevitable calls for the batting to be reinforced. Dexter, the natural beneficiary of any such move, had not, however, been distinguishing himself off the field. 'I really had no idea of what a twelfth man had to do. I thought that all I had to do was hang around when we were fielding and trot on if anyone had to leave the field. I had never before acted as twelfth man and I had no clue about drinks and towels and drying clothes.' It gets worse. Dexter admits to 'terrible performances as twelfth man' and explains: 'I remember spending a good deal of my time, certainly in the lunch intervals, jugging it up and having marvellous oyster parties when I should have been looking after the boys.' Quite what his reaction would have been as chairman of the England committee, had he found the nominated twelfth man in the champagne tent at Lord's one day, is difficult to judge. But Dexter does not try to spare his own blushes

52

about his behaviour. 'It was my first tour abroad and in horse-racing terms I needed a pair of blinkers to keep my mind on the job . . . I was totally ignorant and incompetent and it was probably my incompetence that led to my being selected for the Third Test. They couldn't face the idea of having me as twelfth man again.'

However much of that is true, players on both teams were treating Dexter with something between suspicion and amusement. His natural detachment was still a mystery to most and that he had arrived late, and still made no apparent effort to communicate, did not endear him to all. There were some renowned mickey-takers among the England players, Peter Richardson prominent among them, and Dexter became an obvious target for mirth. The Australians, too, did not spare him and Benaud confirms the oft-related story of what was said when, on the first afternoon of the Sydney Test, he arrived at the crease with England in trouble again at 97 for four. 'I was at slip for Slater when Ted came in,' recalls Benaud, 'and he asked, in what seemed a very upper-class voice not in keeping with "Yabba's Hill", for "two laigs, please". Wally Grout turned to me and said, quite loudly enough to bring Ted's head around a little, "blue-blooded ones, of course . . ." The sledging was a little more subtle in those days.'

Grout and company had no time to develop the theme or draw any further conclusions about the newcomer. Slater quickly had Dexter leg-before for one, with a slower off-spinner, and England slid towards another inadequate total, another first-innings deficit. Rain, however, had cut two sessions from the second day and a six-hour century by Colin Cowdrey averted any prospect of the series being lost in the equivalent of straight sets, but for Dexter, the game had no happy endings. He managed 11 in the second innings, caught Grout bowled Benaud, and with a dropped catch also in the debit column, he was not remotely surprised to be stood down again for the next match in Adelaide.

It made no difference. England, against most expectations, were being thoroughly outclassed by a well-drilled Australian side in which Benaud himself was an outstanding influence both as captain and chief wicket-taker. His leg-breaks had accounted for seven English wickets in Brisbane and nine in Sydney. He added a further nine in Adelaide, and England, now with Fred Trueman and Frank Tyson in a reshuffled side, were humbled by ten wickets.

The pack was shuffled again for the final Test, academic in terms of the series but important, as ever, in Ashes esteem. Trevor Bailey played the last Test of his career and, opening the innings, was out for nought in each innings to Ray Lindwall. And Dexter returned with a first-ball 'duck' and a scratchy hour for 6. Australia won by nine wickets, took the series 4–0 and gave rise to some withering criticism of an England side which had held the Ashes for three consecutive series but, now, had lost them in resounding fashion.

Dexter was singled out, not only because he had failed, for he was not alone in that, but because he had arrived with a lofty reputation and had been labelled as an archetypal Englishman of a type the Australians love to deride. 'Very upright, very British, very vulnerable,' was how one writer succinctly described his impressions of Dexter, but not everyone was so polite. One story that created headlines claimed that he had been asked to leave a prestigious Melbourne hotel for being improperly dressed. The vision of Dexter improperly dressed was irresistible to the Australians and they made great capital out of it. Dexter, while not denying the incident, describes it somewhat less dramatically. On a hot day, he had been looking for someone in the England party and had ventured into the dining room in shorts and sandals. On being asked to conform to regulations by putting on a jacket, he tried to explain his business but eventually left. Somehow this minor altercation was transmitted to a newspaper office, with the inevitable outcome.

But if there was a constant temptation to ridicule Dexter's image, there were also those prepared to crucify his cricketing pretensions. One of the foremost Australian cricket writers of the day was A. G. Moyes and his summary of Dexter's tour could scarcely have been more damning. 'On the form he showed,' wrote Moyes, 'he was one of the poorest batsmen to appear in a Test in Australia in the past forty years. As a bowler Dexter was not even a good third change when it came to Test cricket and his throwing lacked speed and accuracy. One can only wonder why there was such an agitation in some quarters to have him sent out as a replacement.'

Throughout his life Dexter has given the appearance of being immune to such barbs. Like his alleged arrogance, it is a mistaken impression. He never has been insensitive and, in early 1959, he was desperately unhappy to be so mocked. 'I had been the buffoon of the party,' he confessed later. But it did not make it any easier to accept other people telling him so in print.

There were genuine reasons for his poor performance. Late-comers take time to adjust to a touring party in which the main group is already comfortably acclimatized and unified. The pro-tracted journey did not help, or his poor health. And he was so patently out of practice that bad habits crept, undetected, into his game, habits that needed to be identified by a third party. As the team was scheduled to travel on to New Zealand for two more Tests in March, Dexter headed purposefully for the nets, where salvation awaited him. 'It was John Mortimore who spotted my failing. He told me that I was batting with the face of the bat open. Initially, I protested but then I turned the bat a little in my hands and immediately the timing was right and I was hitting the ball properly again.'

Such minor but essential technical repairs have rescued many an ailing career and Dexter was suitably grateful for Mortimore's observations. When the first Test against New Zealand began at Lancaster Park, the unlovely rugby stadium on the outskirts of lovely Christchurch, May won the toss and batted. By the close of the first day Dexter was 123 not out. He went on to make 141 and New Zealand, little more resilient than they had been in England the previous summer, were once more beaten by an innings. A fortnight later in Auckland, the weather was so unpleasant that play on the first two days was frequently halted because the wind had blown off the bails; play on the last two days was abandoned. Dexter made only one in his single innings but, with only two regular fast bowlers in the side, he had his first long bowl in a Test match and took three wickets for 23. Given the dispiriting events in Australia, it was in relatively buoyant mood that Dexter headed home. 'I felt that I had come of age. There were to be some disappointments ahead, and there was much to learn, but I knew that I had been accepted.'

There was more to the uplifted spirit than a maiden Test century. Dexter was coming home to be married, a fixture that had helped sustain him through some of the darker days of his first tour. The ceremony was conducted by the vicar of Bray and took place on 2 May. The reception, a suitably stylish affair, was held on Monkey Island, on the Maidenhead stretch of the Thames, and when Ted and Susan left that evening, they went by boat and then car to Rye in Sussex, a sentimental overnight stop in the town where Ted had helped win the Varsity golf match the previous year and Susan had lent moral support.

The next day, the newly-weds took a ferry to France and began the honeymoon proper. It was not, perhaps, the glamorous interlude one might expect. Ted was close to broke. He had borrowed a car for the holiday and had £100 to spend. After little over a week, that money had gone and the Dexters travelled back across the Channel to set up their first home, a flat in Ebury Street, Victoria, given to them as a wedding present by Ted's father Ralph.

The new cricket season was already under way and Dexter hoped to establish his England place beyond question during the five-Test series against India. But the summer did not proceed to plan and he was chosen for none of the first three games, all won by embarrassing margins by England. By the time he was recalled at Old Trafford, precisely twelve months after he had made his début on the same ground, the only remaining competitive element revolved around whether England could gain five wins in a series for the first time. They duly did so, without fuss, but Dexter's part was small and as the season ended he went back into the world of insurance with a heavy heart.

Susan was earning good money, far more than her husband, for she was a sought-after fashion model in London. Dexter became depressed by his own lack of direction and, during three idle months in the offices of a city insurance broker who could find him nothing productive to do, he developed an interest in the turf that has remained with him but which, at the time, threatened to take him over. Oddly, Ted had not been greatly drawn to horse-racing in his university days, despite mixing with plenty of Newmarket trainers at Worlington golf club. Seeds had undoubtedly been sown in his mind, however, and it did not take much to activate the gambling spirit which lay dormant within him. All it took was time on his hands to study the racing press during office hours. Betting offices were nearby and, without even noticing it at first, he began to bet dangerously heavily. 'I started on the road to near ruin,' he recalled. 'Gambling ran in the family to some degree but, whereas my father was a small-scale punter with a large income, I did things the wrong way round.' It was a slippery slope, made the more treacherous when Dexter con-tracted jaundice. He went through spells of introspection and depression, in which he questioned his future profoundly. What rescued him was a tour of the West Indies on which he proved to all that he could be one of the great batsmen of his day, and his simultaneous appointment to a new and diverting challenge, as captain of Sussex.

Chapter Four

If any one year can be said to have been the making of Ted Dexter's cricket career, it is surely 1960, for it had at least as much potential to break him. Dexter might still have been unsure of cricket as a calling when he set off for the West Indies with the MCC touring party at the start of the year; those who sit in judgement on such matters were certainly unsure of him and some offered the firm view that he had no place there.

Come the end of the summer, nine months on, such mutual doubts were forgotten. Dexter was not only a fixture at number three for England, acknowledged even by those who had previously derided him as a masterly player of fast bowling; he had also confounded many a sceptical forecast by making an outstanding success of his first season in charge of the Sussex team. Through the history of the game, this is a mission that has seldom been guaranteed to bring any reflected glory and Dexter had taken on the job with the team, and the club, at a particularly low ebb in their fortunes. The personality, panache and – at least at first – the drive he brought to Hove contrived a remarkable transformation.

The depressions of twelve months earlier now seemed to belong to another life and another, less assertive character. Here, surely, was a man of his age, a compelling cavalier of a sportsman, the devil-may-care approach concealing a tigerish resolution. Well, anyway, this was how the newspapers of the day had begun to describe him and how the ad-men, in this coming commercial era, were prone to portray one of few cricketers they deemed worthy of interest. All in all, it was, as Dexter recalled, 'the start of an all too brief period when critics were disposed to say nice things about me'.

It was an unfamiliar party that toured the Caribbean that year, or, more accurately, it was a party shorn of the most familiar faces of preceding years. Bailey, Evans, Laker and Tyson had all given way to youth. Peter May was captain and, prior to departure by ship, he described his team as 'young and experimental'. May, Colin Cowdrey, Fred Trueman and Brian Statham were the stalwarts of the mission but many were still in the infancy of their England careers. Among those making their first tour were Ray Illingworth, M. J. K. Smith and E. R. Dexter.

There is a rose-tinted retrospective to Dexter's career, an impression that it was always Lord's in the June sunshine and that Lord Edward was forever, by royal decree, batting at number three and hitting Wes Hall on the up through extra-cover. There is a popular, parallel judgement on his life, which is generally assumed to be one of privilege and entitlement, in which success was not so much an achievement as a natural progression. Dexter's hauteur has not discouraged such presumption but the facts tell a rather different story.

He was, for instance, neither an automatic nor a universally approved choice for that West Indies tour. Plenty remembered his gormless efforts in Australia a year earlier; plenty more, in the fashion the English adopt to denigrate their most talented individuals, thought Dexter was living on an unearned reputation. Just as pertinently, in that time of change towards a more professional class of English cricketers, Dexter was regarded as a slightly unwelcome throwback. In his book on the tour, *Through the Caribbean*, journalist Alan Ross described Dexter as 'an aloof all-rounder whose selection had not pleased the popular pundits who saw in it a predilection for amateurs'.

This barbed and unjustified prejudice followed Dexter throughout his time in cricket. Almost everything he did was, in some quarters, compromised by a view that he was a dilettante dipping his bread into every available dish of consommé yet seldom finishing the meal. Dexter's breadth of interests and ambitions lent credence to the suspicion that he would be here today and gone tomorrow, yet it was not always so, for he has also been obsessive, identifying a target that fascinates him and then pursuing it single-mindedly.

Once he had come to terms with the demands of Test cricket, he approached it in this calculating way. But that had not happened on his first, disillusioning tour or during the summer of 1959, the events of which had set him on course for his depressed autumn. He had not, up to then, gained the acceptance at Test level which many had believed inevitable and there is no doubt that the West Indies series was a watershed for him.

M. J. K. Smith had been two years ahead of Dexter at university and his last Varsity Match was Ted's first. Smith, captaining Oxford and batting as Dexter's opposite number at four, made a century in the drawn match of 1956. Dexter's contribution was relatively mundane but he made an impression on Smith, none the less. 'He was so very orthodox in technique,' he recalls. 'School pitches start everyone off on the front foot but Cyril Coote, at Fenner's, had got Ted playing off the back foot in the way all good players must but very few young players can. He had something special and, as soon as he turned up anywhere, he attracted attention. It was always that way with Ted.'

But Smith, whose selection for the West Indies was never in serious doubt, well remembers that the Dexter star was not quite in the ascendancy during 1959. During that summer, England's selectors tampered endlessly with their batting order, giving caps to Arthur Milton, Ken Taylor, Martin Horton and even Gilbert Parkhouse, who had last played eight years earlier. It was not until the fourth Test against India that Dexter was recalled and he hardly advertised his credentials to tour by making 13, 45 and 0 in the three innings available to him. 'He was a borderline case for the tour,' confirms Smith, 'and, when we got there, he won the last batting place for the first Test in Barbados.'

A good thing he did. Against an attack including Wes Hall, Frank Worrell, Sonny Ramadhin and Garry Sobers, Dexter established himself beyond argument with an innings of 136 not out.

The power and grandeur of strokeplay one associates with Dexter was readily apparent, but so, too, was a resolution not always previously evident. He batted through one day and into another, remaining undefeated when the innings ended. He gave one, difficult chance and showed no intention of offering any more. The match meandered towards stalemate, Sobers and Worrell putting on 399 for the West Indies' fourth wicket and England barely beginning their second innings at the fag-end of the final day. No matter, Dexter was now an England batsman, prospectively a great one.

Of all the Test matches he was subsequently to play, few were as turbulent or controversial as the next, at Port of Spain. It included rumblings of a bouncer war – yes, thirty-five years ago – and an alarming crowd riot. Dexter was at the focus of both and he made the critical contribution as England secured a wholly unexpected victory on the sixth and final day.

This was a match that began burdened by the pressures of racial and parochial resentments which, to a lesser degree, still plague West Indian cricket today. Gerry Alexander, a light-skinned Jamaican, was captaining West Indies ahead of Frank Worrell, a situation described in a daily newspaper by the influential C. L. R. James as 'revolting'. More revolting, to some objective eyes, was the custom in the Caribbean of choosing locally acceptable players. For this Trinidad game, for instance, two Jamaicans, Easton McMorris and Reg Scarlett, were dropped and flew home immediately complaining of the hostile attentions of the Trinidad public. In Scarlett's place, as the second spinner to local hero Sonny Ramadhin, was installed one Charran Singh, a twenty-one-year-old messenger-boy from the Trinidad outpost of San Juan. He had played scarcely any first-class cricket, and played little more, but his début was warmly applauded locally, where interest in the game was at fever pitch. Given what was to follow, this home-town selection by the West Indies understandably found less favour with the England party and, particularly, with Dexter.

Before Singh's gentle left-arm spin could play any part, the mood of the match was set by a stream of short balls from Hall

61

and Chester Watson. Ken Barrington was the principal sufferer, felled by a bouncer from Hall that took him behind the ear. He beat the count, ever the willing pugilist, and was 93 not out overnight, but at breakfast on the second morning he came out with a prophetic comment. 'Crash helmets will be worn,' he said, and a little less than twenty years on, he was proved right.

Dexter had scored 77 on the first day. He had entered at number five, promotion of one place in the order, when Hall and Watson had reduced England to 57 for three. As Alan Ross wrote:

> Few fast bowlers could have kept up such pace over a whole morning. It was an onslaught much the same as they had produced at Bridgetown, and even more successful. But Dexter wasn't having any of it. He drove Hall in his first over through mid-on and crashed him on the rise past cover. He appeared as cool and detached as a De Reszke cigarette advertisement.

But Dexter was out to Singh, giving the youngster his first Test wicket with a return catch, and if he felt some sense of retribution (which he probably did not) when he ran out the débutant with a smart throw from cover on the third afternoon, it was soon replaced by a baser instinct – self-preservation – as the capacity crowd of 22,000 reacted violently.

At the time, West Indies were 98 for eight in reply to England's total of 382. Dismay, and the scent of unacceptable defeat, were powerful influences but, in the mind of Michael Manley, not the only influences. Manley, who became prime minister of Jamaica in 1972, laments the affair in his *A History of West Indies Cricket*:

> Although play was stopped, tear gas employed and the English team escorted from the field, the eruption was not directed against the visiting players but against the West Indian umpire who gave the West Indian spinner out. Judged from one point of view it was a disgraceful episode; looked at from another, it was symptomatic of the sometimes self-destructive, inwardly focused tensions in the society . . . But

worse than that, the side was losing. In the end both the decision and the unsuccessful context provided by the game were probably no more than catalysts serving to release other tensions with other causes. The thought that a West Indian figure of authority, the umpire, could in any way contribute to a heightening of the collective shame of failure seemed to trigger the only response available to the people on the spot. Irrationally and with overpowering crudeness they lost their tempers.

M. J. K. Smith's view corresponds: 'We had gone two days without taking a wicket in Barbados and the crowd turned up, that day in Port of Spain, expecting to watch the West Indies plaster us around the ground. Instead, Fred [Trueman] and Brian [Statham] bowled them out. Their frustration grew, quite noticeably, and by late afternoon, when it was stinking hot and most of them had had a drink and lost all their bets, they had seen enough. The run-out was just an excuse.

'Although we had to beat a retreat, I never felt we were personally in any great danger. I remember one spectator running past me saying, "We're not after you, we're after those umpires."'

There were thirty hospital cases and another sixty were treated for minor injuries. There could be no further cricket that day. But once emotions had cooled, a decision was taken to add an extra day on to the game, which persuaded Peter May not to enforce the follow-on, despite a lead of 270. England stretched that advantage to 500 – Dexter out for nought, bowled by Hall – and allowed ten hours to bowl out the West Indies for a second time, but in mid-afternoon on the last day they were 222 for five, Rohan Kanhai defiantly past 100. It was then that Dexter, called upon to bowl for the first time in the match, made the vital breach. Mike Smith relates: 'I never thought Ted could do a front-line bowler's job. His knees were dodgy, of course, but also I didn't think his bowling was up to it. But he was a very handy man to have up your sleeve and many is the time he would break partnerships at important moments. This was one of them. Ted bowled a harmless full-toss on Rohan's legs and he hit it straight to me at mid-wicket.'

Such are the moments which reflect a man's fortunes and Dexter's were undeniably soaring. As that tour proceeded, the Midas touch remained loyal. England won a series in the West Indies for the first time by drawing the three remaining Tests and Ted not only finished top of the Test batting averages, winning from *Wisden* the compliment of having 'thoroughly justified the faith of the selectors in choosing him', he also continued his climb of the batting order and, through mishaps to others, took root at number three.

First, Peter May had to go home for further treatment to an internal wound, aggravated since a pre-tour operation and concealed from the rest of the party by a mix of bravery and misguided selflessness. Then, during the fourth Test at Georgetown, in what was still British Guiana, Ken Barrington, a particular target for the short-pitched bowling, was hit above the elbow by Wes Hall. He dropped down the order for the second innings and his place, that pivotal place occupied down the years by only the best batsmen, passed to the young pretender. Dexter responded by making 110, stifling West Indies' victory ambitions after they had led on first innings by 107. According to Alan Ross, he 'had looked more the part of a classical number three than anyone on view for a long time'.

The MCC party returned in triumph and none was more triumphant than Dexter. West Indies tours traditionally being staged in the English spring, he now had to report immediately to Hove and a new, quite different challenge in the role for which Robin Marlar had identified him four years earlier. Against his own will and judgement, Marlar had done one final year as Sussex captain in 1959. 'It was a mistake,' he admits. 'We had a terrible year and with hindsight I should have stuck to my guns. But some of the committee had been upset by what they believed to be Ted's cavalier attitude – the Copenhagen incident still rankled – and they said they wanted the Sussex public to get used to him first.' What

Brushed, scrubbed and barely out of short trousers . . . an early portrait of Ted (*right*), and (*below*) flanked by his mother and father in a family group, with elder brother John third from the right. (*Ted Dexter*)

Dexter as captain of the unbeaten 1953 Radley First XI. (*Radley College*)

Opposite: In 1958, his final year at Cambridge, Dexter is captain of the university and awaiting his first Test call.

Left: A grimly determined Dexter on his way to making 52 on Test debut against New Zealand at Old Trafford.

Opposite: Then, as now, Ted would seldom pass up the chance of a day at the races. Top-hatted and tailed for Oaks day at Epsom, 1961.

Below: In this moment England's Ashes quest of 1961 foundered. Dexter's outrageous 76 at Old Trafford is ended by Richie Benaud, bowling his leg-spin round the wicket.

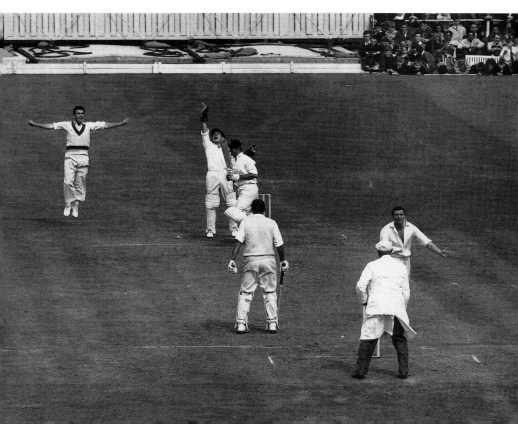

Dexter knocks back the off stump of his rival captain, Frank Worrell, in the Edgbaston Test of 1963. (*Ken Kelly*)

Opposite: It was usually other people who held the cameras when Ted and Susan appeared together. Here, fashionable as ever, on the seafront at Glenelg, Adelaide, on the 1962–63 tour of Australia.

No need for the umpire's finger. Dexter caught behind off Garry Sobers in the 1963 Oval Test.

Toasting the fans at the end of a memorable series against the West Indies, a new force in world cricket.

they probably meant, Marlar knew, was that they had to get used to Dexter.

Sussex, as a county, was not unused to star quality. How could it be, when Ranji, C. B. Fry and Percy Fender numbered among the old boys? But Dexter was something else. With him, it was timing as much as anything, for he descended upon Hove with a club prone to somnolence pretty much asleep on its feet, and although anyone who has met or known him would vouch that Dexter is far from being a loud or demonstrative man, he is impossible to ignore. The aura that has hung about him his entire life was now to transform Sussex, instilling ambition and creating untold success. If it was, sadly, only short term, it was in character with the fleeting triumphs of Dexter's butterfly existence.

Hove is a changeless ground. The cast-list may have altered down the years, the rate of achievement fluctuated, but the Hove one sees today, with its long, low members' pavilion to the west, its deckchairs enticingly placed at the top of the ground, traditional scoreboards on each square boundary, is pretty much as it was thirty-five years ago. The seaward vista has been obstructed by the erection of a block of flats but, otherwise, it is the same, pleasingly dozy scene into which Edward Ralph Dexter swung his pale blue Jaguar SS100 in April of 1960, having by then outgrown an Anglia and a Borgward.

He had returned from West Indies with his playing reputation restored and his celebrity status enhanced. Charisma surrounded him. Along with his stunning wife, he cut such a dashing, mus-keteer figure that the inevitable his-and-hers modelling offers arrived. So, too, of course, did any number of society invitations of a sort not normally handled by county cricketers. With his – at least superficially – easy manner, his charm and breeding, Dexter suited any company, which is one good reason why certain members of the Sussex committee were intimidated by him. Robin Marlar was not prone to being intimidated. Or to feeling remotely outclassed. As librarian to the Duke of Norfolk, he mixed with genuine aristocrats rather than those, like Dexter, who were merely of aristocratic bearing. Now that he had handed over the club captaincy he had no patience with any who still hankered for the quiet life. 'I had found Ted to be both responsive and responsible while I was captain,' reported Marlar, 'and I did not have the slightest doubt that he would do the job well. In fact, I looked forward to seeing how he would shake things up.'

This 'shake-up' was plainly necessary. Since finishing second, for the sixth time, in 1953, Sussex had been mere also-rans in the title race they had not once won. Between 1956 and 1959 they finished ninth twice, thirteenth and then fifteenth, and while Surrey gave way to Yorkshire after winning the championship seven times in succession, the notion that Sussex might feature at the prizegiving was nothing short of risible. As Marlar explains: 'The atmosphere of Sussex cricket in those days wasn't attuned to winning. The club was into entertainment, and nurturing cricketers' careers, but it seemed bizarre to us to start a championship season feeling we had to win it. At that time, we were in the majority, and it was this attitude, which would now seem complacent and unambitious, that Ted was landed with.'

When the mood takes him, and a particular challenge diverts that complex mind, Dexter can be a dynamic figure and, buoyed by his experiences in the Caribbean and determined to make a good fist of the next thing on his cricketing agenda, Dexter swept into the new season like a typhoon. In later years, he acknowledged that he attained heights in those few weeks that were thereafter beyond him in championship cricket, for its sheer, relentless demands on mind and body inevitably blunted his edge. But 1960 was very special.

The following year's *Wisden* recorded the facts with more admiration than was traditional in its flat delivery. 'That Sussex accomplished the remarkably steep ascent from fifteenth place in the Championship table in 1959 to fourth last summer was due in no small measure to their new captain, Dexter, who proved a considerable inspiration to the side,' the good book intoned. And so he did.

Sussex played 32 championship games that year (some counties had only 28 and the title was decided by a points-per-game average) and won twelve. This was a fine advance in itself but, come the end of May, there had been a genuine danger of blood-pressure casualties among the deckchair brigade as Sussex threatened to carry all before them in a quite unprecedented fashion.

Dexter's love of theory can sometimes blur and confuse but, at his best, he is splendidly analytical of the technical faults of teams and individuals. M. J. K. Smith believes him to be one of the best batting coaches he has known and still recommends players today to take their troubles to him. In 1960, Dexter identified that one of Sussex's most damaging shortcomings was their failure to hold enough catches. This applied specifically to the slip fielders and Dexter's remedy was to depute Alan Oakman, a renowned close catcher who had played two Tests against Australia in 1956, to put things right. Oakman rose to his duties, supervising sessions of catching practice both pre-season and before play each day, in a way now familiar to all county and international sides but, in those days, foreign to their routine. Dexter, once again, was years ahead of his time, and the success of the theory was there for all to see.

Sussex's opening championship game that year was at Edgbaston, where Warwickshire were led by M. J. K. Smith and had, as a new-ball bowler, Dexter's Cambridge contemporary Ossie Wheatley. They had finished fourth in 1959 and were expected to be too good for Sussex. Perhaps they believed it, for after taking first-innings lead Smith declared before lunch on the third day and asked Sussex to score 255 in just under three hours. Dexter, batting at three, proceeded to thunder 93 in a mere 51 minutes and win the game by six wickets.

The next match, at Taunton, was drawn but Dexter hit a century in 85 minutes and carried his irresistible form on into a game which made the whole country sit up and take notice. Yorkshire arrived at Hove as reigning champions, destined to retain the title. They arrived with a team of names – Illingworth, Trueman and Close to the fore – and looked at first as if they would toy with these south-coast upstarts. Despite 96 from Dexter, Sussex managed only 280 and Yorkshire passed it without losing a wicket before, somewhat patronizingly, declaring directly. But when Sussex went in again, Dexter made another 76 and then audaciously declared, asking Yorkshire to make 250 in 155 minutes. This was not the cosy complacency they were used to at Hove: here was a captain going headlong in pursuit of victory – and against the best side in England. That they managed it, bowling out Yorkshire for 217, said much for the self-belief that Dexter had, in a remarkably short space of time, instilled in his players.

Glamorgan and Nottinghamshire were quickly seen off in consecutive home games, whereupon Sussex embarked on a double-header, away and then home, against Surrey, neighbours who had dominated them for years. Not this time, however. At the Oval, play was only possible on the first day and it was monopolized by Sussex, Dexter making 104 out of 327 for four against an attack which comprised the Bedser twins, Peter Loader, David Gibson and Tony Lock. If the weather reprieved Surrey there, they found no bolt-holes at Hove, where Don Bates – a seasoned seam bowler totally rejuvenated by Dexter – and Tony Buss bowled them out for 158 and 254. Sussex needed to bat only the once, Dexter making 135 and Jim Parks 155 out of 451 for five. Alec Bedser's figures were nought for 81, Lock's were one for 113 and Surrey retreated up the A23 with a rare and resounding innings defeat.

Sussex, then, had played seven championship games in May, drawing two and winning the rest. It was a phenomenal start, too good to be maintained, but the members, who were mushrooming rapidly in number, had every reason to feel euphoric. Simply defeating Surrey – for the first time since 1947 – was enough to satisfy many.

As the summer, a wet and sunless one, continued, the distractions mounted for Dexter, for he was now an automatic choice at number three in the Test side and played in the entire five-match series against South Africa. It was an unsatisfactory affair, not only because England settled it by winning the first three Tests against disappointing opposition but because the Lord's Test, and thus the series itself, was dominated by a throwing controversy. Geoff Griffin, the South African involved, had quite a match, for not only was he the first man to be no-balled for throwing in a Test match in England, he also became the first man to do the hat-trick in a Lord's Test. He never played Test cricket again.

Dexter went through the series without a century and averaged only 26. In this one year, indeed, his memorable cricket was played for Sussex, none better than in a remarkable victory over Middlesex in early August. Sussex ruled the match throughout, Dexter scoring 157 as they attained a first-innings lead of 147 and declaring for a second time to set the visitors 329 on the last day. They were never in the hunt and Dexter, galvanizing his bowling arm, had taken three for one to reduce Middlesex to 121 for six when a storm broke over Hove. An hour remained when the game resumed and Dexter took two more wickets with consecutive balls before the Middlesex tail-enders mounted a monumental rearguard action and 82 dot-balls ensued. Inevitably, in this of all summers, it was Dexter who made the breach and a brilliant close catch which helped him. His figures then were 6 for one in eight overs and there were those around the county who had begun to believe he was capable of almost anything.

Following that victory over Middlesex, who were still in the title hunt, Sussex retained an outside chance of breaking their championship duck. That notion went astray during Eastbourne week, when Dexter was absent on England duty and the side failed to glean a single point from their two games. But the eventual fourth place was still rightly acclaimed as a considerable achievement and the atmosphere generated by Dexter was mirrored in the addition of 1200 members to the county books.

If anything summed up Dexter in 1960 it was that fading anachronism, the Gentlemen versus Players match at Lord's. Like much else during the summer it was grievously rain-affected and contrivance was needed to make a contest of it, the Players being asked to score 168 in 105 minutes. Dexter had made no impact on the game, making nought and 7 and taking only one wicket, and yet, as David Allen and Alan Moss turned for the second run needed for victory off the final ball of the game, it was Dexter who threw out the middle stump from long-on to leave the game drawn, scores level.

Wisden made Dexter one of their five Cricketers of the Year and it was as much for his achievements at Sussex as for his emergence, in the West Indies, as a formidable Test player. Robin Marlar wrote the tribute to Dexter in the 1961 edition of the cricketing bible and was fulsome in his admiration. 'Our film star, the Cambridge golfers called him,' recalled Marlar, 'but try and stop a drive and you will know that this is not a mere celluloid hero.'

Marlar was not the first to begin comparisons with the great Australian Keith Miller, and to concentrate them on the style of his bowling, described by Marlar as 'speed unleashed in a final orgy of muscular activity'. Dexter modestly disclaimed the similarity, claiming that he was preoccupied by fighting for his batting place in the Test side. But he would have liked one line especially from Marlar's article and, in 1960, few would have disputed it. 'No English cricketer bred since the war has so captured the imagination of those inside, outside and far from the boundary ropes of our big cricket grounds.'

Chapter Five

Limited-overs cricket is nowadays played in such volume that it requires a serious effort to recall that as recently as the 1960s it was regarded with grave suspicion, kept at bay far longer than was desirable and then, when the barrier finally came down under pressure, dismissed by many as the road to ruin.

If the single source for judgement is the correctness of techniques and their effect on batting and bowling standards, those diehard doomtellers had quite a point. But, of course, it is not. One-day cricket has to be gauged by its impact on the game's popularity and profile and, once viewed through this wide lens, there is no room for doubting its force for good. Like any radical innovation, however, it needed time to be appreciated and understood, not only by those on the outside looking in but also by those whose terms of employment were suddenly and rudely broadened to include the playing of these instant matches.

To many of the players of the early 1960s, it was a matter of little consequence – an irritant, maybe, in that it involved a few more days of fairly energetic activity, but nothing more serious than that. They did not consider it important or influential so they did not make the adjustments necessary to play it successfully. There were a few exceptions to this but easily the most striking was Ted Dexter. He had identified the public appeal of one-day cricket even before the Gillette Cup came along and, when it did, he had evolved a way of playing it that was to be immensely beneficial to Sussex. It was, indeed, to put their name on county cricket's honours board for the first time in their history.

It would be wrong to believe that Dexter revelled in limited-overs cricket. Though it fulfilled him to achieve what he set out to do for Sussex, he found that the one-day game, played under the rules existing at the time, was a licence to be negative. 'It simply made for stereotyped seam bowling,' he explains. 'Sussex won their two Gillette Cups before the other counties had woken up to the problem.' But whether he liked it or not, Dexter understood what it took to succeed at the shorter game. He also understood why it was necessary, perhaps essential, to play it – and market it – to arrest an alarming decline in attendances at county cricket and to deflect the notion, regularly raised but truer then than on most similar occasions, that cricket was dying through lack of interest.

It was not as simplistic as that, of course. If the game was dying – and the figures certainly made grim reading – then it was more through lack of dynamic direction than lack of interest. Other sports, and leisure outlets, were now gathering support through their own endeavours, like politicians electioneering in the streets. Cricket, and the majority of cricket administrators, still believed that the votes would come their way as of right.

These years of revolution within the sport were to see both the end of the amateur player and the giant step into the unknown epitomized by the 1963 Gillette Cup. It had been spawned, however, by the success of a series of Sunday limited-overs matches, sponsored by Rothman's and featuring many of the most attractive cricketers of the day. They were appropriately named the International Cavaliers and they appropriately included E. R. Dexter. Here, at first hand, Dexter absorbed the lessons of the experiment, saw how limited-overs cricket could be made to work in the playing sense and as an entrepreneurial event. He saw the light, long before most of his contemporaries, that cricket had to compete commercially. Maybe it was this realization that awakened within him the idea of operating his own public-relations company in the sporting field.

At that time, of course, Dexter was an amateur – one of the more genuine amateurs but nevertheless capable of commanding considerable sums of money through his cricketing ability. The same arguments that rugby union waited thirty years to address, athletics almost as long, now confronted cricket as an anomaly because in cricket, as opposed to the other named sports, the remnants of the amateur era were playing with and against a majority who openly made their living from the sport. The lingering distinctions were distasteful to many and vocally resented by the more militant of the professionals, who failed to see why people who could afford to play for nothing – or at least ostensibly for nothing – should be pampered with preferential facilities.

It was, plainly, a nonsense, but not everyone agreed it was time for change. The 1963 *Wisden* greeted the abolition of the outdated status with alarm: 'By doing away with the amateur, cricket is in danger of losing the spirit of freedom and gaiety which the best amateur players brought to the game.'

Wisden's point was that amateurs, playing because they wanted to rather than because they needed to, could express their talent without fear or inhibition. It is an argument that has regained favour in more recent times, when the relentless nature of the modern game has sometimes seemed to stifle free spirits. There were those who believed David Gower should have continued playing as a part-timer when he diverted into the media, and that Phillip Edmonds' notion of mixing a career in the City with a spot of dilettante county cricket had merit. The same case was made for Ted Dexter on his premature retirement. But all this is to confuse part-time with amateur, or with what, in the early 1960s, passed for amateur.

Dexter believed they were all 'shamateurs', and had no hesitation in saying so. The same point was made by Michael Melford, writing in the *Daily Telegraph* on 26 November 1962, after the first-class counties had voted to abolish the distinction. 'One does not have to be any sort of a revolutionary to feel that the right decision has been made,' commented Melford. 'The time had come when the successful amateur, by writing and advertising, was making so much money out of cricket that a form of legalized deceit was being practised.'

It was also a divisive distinction, one good reason for its abolition. Robin Marlar explains: 'You must remember that social divisions were very clear in cricket. It was all very different from how it is now. After a day's play at Hove, the professionals would gather and go off to the Palais after the amateurs had said goodbye in the pub at the bottom of the ground and gone home to their wives. Ted came in as the amateurs were on their way out; he was the last amateur at Sussex. But it suited him because he was never one of the boys, anyway. Everybody would be his friend and yet he was close to nobody.'

Alan Oakman, who observed Dexter's descent on Sussex with interest and amusement, reflects: 'I often thought he would have been better off playing in the 1930s. The style and pace of those days would have suited him so much more. I can see him with his MCC tie round his waist, holding up his flannels.'

But if Dexter belonged in the Corinthian age, he did not mourn its passing. It meant an end to the Gentlemen versus Players match, and to separate dressing rooms, but otherwise it made little difference to him that he was now of the same status as every other cricketer. For, evidently, he would never be of the same outlook as the majority, or of the same ability.

The fall of the amateur and the rise of the Gillette Cup were coincidentally linked, yet both were indications of the growing financial awareness in cricket. It took many more years to filter and permeate until outright commercialism was prevalent, but these were the infant steps, wobbly and uncertain, towards revolution. The game in England would never be the same again. Sussex, dear old Sussex who had never flown the championship pennant in all their long and colourful history, won the Gillette Cup in each of its first two years. It was an unimaginable triumph in a competition that not only invigorated the club but the game itself, creating such an unconsidered level of interest that it became obvious to even the sceptics – of whom there remained many – that the measured tread of the county circuit was to be irretrievably altered. Quite how far, nobody could then conceive.

What is generally agreed is that the Sussex triumphs in the

Gillette were also personal triumphs for Dexter. He was an un-orthodox and potentially infuriating county captain, as we shall see later, but this new challenge was very much his kind of thing. As Robin Marlar says: 'Ted had inherited an unambitious set-up and the Gillette gave him a heaven-sent opportunity to shape a success. It was his crowning achievement as county captain, because he was innovative in his field-settings and his use of differ-ent players, and he comprehended what it was all about.'

Alan Oakman agrees. 'Ted had come to us full of energy but over the years he lost interest in county cricket. The Gillette was a different matter, though. He was full of enthusiasm and ideas when it came to the one-day games and I believe you can put our success in the Cup down to him.'

It might be – and has been – cynically suggested that Dexter's enthusiasm for the one-day game sprang from the knowledge that it gave him two days off. Certainly, this was the way of it with some county players of the day. But for Dexter it was more than a free pass to the racecourse: it was a stimulant, something on which to exercise the brain cells which had begun to stagnate on the monotonous diet of three-day cricket to half-empty grounds. Here was a stage on which to perform – and, it soon became clear, a substantial audience to perform to.

The predominant feeling around the counties when agreement was reached for the Gillette to begin was not excitement but curi-osity. There were some discontented rumblings from the players, until they realized that, short-term at least, it would lessen their workload rather than increase it. And there was naturally some interest from the county treasurers, hard-pressed to a man follow-ing years of steady decline in membership levels and attendances. But no one could be sure what the impact would be, or even if the experiment would survive beyond its initial year.

The early 1960s saw all manner of theorizing over the future of the domestic game. Some was pragmatic, some hopelessly fanciful but every theory advertised a theme of restlessness with a schedule which had been essentially unchanged for too long. The sporting world was moving on – but in which direction? The 1963 *Wisden* contained a lengthy article entitled 'Through The Crystal Ball', hypothesizing about the county cricket ground of the future as 'a comprehensive sports centre' (something which has still not occurred, more than three decades on). But the writer, John Solan, while admitting that 'it remains to be seen whether the knockout competition is going to give a fillip to the county game' warmed to his personal theme thus:

> Week-end county cricket would fall naturally into the general scheme but there would also be the occasional 'celebrity' match with the club playing a side of all the talents . . . Cricketers cast in the mould of Dexter could demand a rich fee from the more prosperous clubs, and other universal personalities could lend variety.

In a sense, this idea was already obsolete. The Rothman's Cavaliers had filled this gap in the market and confirmed that there was potential in the promotion of instant cricket, where the attraction to the non-connoisseur was to see both teams bat, and achieve a result, within a single day. If, along the way, the batting was also designed to entertain, as opposed to the worthy and necessary accumulations of the longer game, so much the better. The Cavaliers had shown the way and, now, cricket had no need of celebrity contrivance, for it was to stage its own sideshow. Not everyone approved. *Wisden* was so doubtful that, for the first year, it declined to acknowledge the Gillette Cup by name, referring to it simply as the Knockout Competition. But when 25,000 packed Lord's for the first final, such condescension had to be dropped. 'At Lord's,' reported *Wisden*, 'supporters wore favours and banners were also in evidence, the whole scene resembling an Association Football final more than the game of cricket and many thousands invaded the pitch at the finish to cheer Dexter, the Sussex captain, as he received the Gillette trophy from the MCC president, Lord Nugent.'

There were no Minor Counties in the competition, that first year, and it was also played over 65 overs per side, with a 15-over restriction on each bowler. The rules were fine-tuned as the event

76

expanded but the most fundamental change was in player-awareness of the different tactics required. Certainly, few seemed aware of them in 1963 and Dexter recalls that Sussex were well advanced towards a total of 314 in their first-round tie at Tunbridge Wells, yet Kent, captained by Colin Cowdrey, were persisting with slip fielders and an attacking strategy. 'Very few teams had thought it through,' explained Alan Oakman. 'It may not say much for the professionals of the day but it is true that, to many of them, the knockout began as a bit of a lark, with the promise of a bit of time off if they got knocked out in the first round.'

Despite Oakman's nought, Sussex built a match-winning score on that late May day among the rhododendrons, and Derek Underwood, who was later to become such a masterful slow bowler for the limited-overs game, conceded 87 runs in 11 overs. Dexter then showed what was to become a familiar hand for the first time, employing five seam bowlers – including the naggingly accurate Ian Thomson and Tony Buss – to field settings designed to contain and frustrate. Kent put up a fight, but fell 72 runs short.

Sussex were second favourites in the next round, when Yorkshire brought their battalion of stars to Hove for a game that attracted a crowd of 15,000. Again, Dexter's tactics were decisive. While most captains, on winning the toss, were choosing to bowl first and then chase a known target, Dexter's view was that it was better to put a score on the board and defend it. Sussex amassed 292, thanks largely to a vivid innings of 90 by Jim Parks, and although Hampshire, Close, Boycott and Balderstone all got going during Yorkshire's reply, Dexter's ambush lay in wait when they tried to force the pace. To widespread surprise, and much joy around Brighton, Yorkshire were vanquished by 22 runs and Sussex proceeded jauntily into the last four, now sure of themselves and, due to Dexter, their tactics.

The semi-final followed a similar course to the two previous games, except that it was less of a contest. 'Win the toss and bat' continued to be Dexter's key to fortune and, although poor Oakman made another nought, Sussex once again topped 290, Dexter and Parks scoring 115 and 71 respectively. Once Colin

Milburn, a man made for this type of cricket, had gone cheaply, Northamptonshire were never in the hunt and Sussex won by a mammoth 105 runs, though long after the other semi-final had been decided in dramatic fashion. Worcestershire dismissed Lancashire for a humiliating 59 to win by nine wickets, knocking off the runs with patronizing speed in 10.1 overs.

The priority later bestowed upon the knockout competitions, perhaps to the unfair detriment of the county championship, was far from evident in 1963 and, having established the two finalists on 10 July, it was not until 7 September that the trophy's destiny was resolved. Eight weeks seemed enough time for cricket followers to lose interest but, instead, the build-up generated ever more attention and, despite cold and drizzly weather on the big day, Lord's could barely have accommodated one more spectator. It was an inspiring sight and, for many of the players, an intimidating one: they had never previously had the opportunity of playing before such a crowd, or for such instant and obviously high stakes. Dexter, to whom Lord's on its great days was almost a second home, might have gone around offering words of comfort and advice but, by all accounts, he did not. It simply wasn't his style. His view was that everyone knew by now what was expected of them and that they should be capable of going out there, enjoying the atmosphere, and doing their job.

In fact, however, there was one man who was not completely familiar with the game-plan, because he had taken no part in the cup-run. He was the twenty-one-year-old son of the vicar of Bognor Regis, fresh out of college with a rebellious streak in him and an ability to bowl fast with enviable control. His name was John Snow and Dexter's decision to give him his knockout début in the final proved inspired.

Winning the toss was not, this time, a passport to prosperity, for these were not free-scoring conditions. But it was not the England seam bowler Jack Flavell – who had destroyed Lancashire in the semi-final – who disrupted Sussex but the left-arm spin of Doug Slade and Norman Gifford, today, ironically, the Sussex cricket manager. Between them they took six Sussex wickets for

56 runs and gave Dexter, who was out for 3, reason to reflect that slow bowling was not necessarily a no-go zone in an overs match.

Sussex had to defend only 168 and Dexter showed that the message had not been lost on him. Although he had his full quota of seam bowlers, he used as first-change the off-breaks of Alan Oakman, and Worcestershire found him impossible to attack. Oakman bowled 13 overs for 17 runs and the priceless wicket of Tom Graveney. Then, with the weather closing in and the September light grim, Dexter showed his uncompromising nature by bringing back his quick bowlers to finish the job. Snow took three for 13 and the ninth wicket fell at 133 but Roy Booth, the Worcestershire wicketkeeper, delayed the celebrations by shielding his number 11 and inching the total up to 154. By now, Dexter had posted every fielder to the boundary, a tactic later outlawed, but its negative intent was fruitful as a run-out in the penultimate over secured victory by a mere 14 runs.

'The match ended in twilight and heavy drizzle,' reported *Wisden*, 'and it was this, coupled with Dexter's superior tactics, which almost certainly cost Worcestershire the match.' John Snow agreed: 'I had never played it before and it was obvious that Ted's tactics upset a few people, but he was within the regulations and he was playing to win. The achievement meant a great deal to everyone at the club, gave us the kudos which goes with success, and as we had also done well in the championship – I think we were still second going into the run-in – there was a sense of purpose and ambition about the place.'

This did not immediately translate into rewards for the players, however, as Oakman recalls. 'The winners' cheque was almost £2,000 but it went straight to the club. We asked the committee about a bonus and were told that they would look after us as usual, which was a bit ominous. Finally, a bonus came through at Christmas. We got £9 each!'

In the following summer, the Gillette began to resemble its eventual form more closely – games were reduced to 60 overs per side to avoid too many finishes in the dark, and five Minor Counties were admitted, though none progressed beyond the first round. For Sussex, business continued as before. Right up to their second final, they batted first in each game and defended their score, though in the third round at Taunton, with only 141 to protect, it was a close-run thing. But at the semi-final stage, while Sussex were making short work of Surrey, the message coming down from Old Trafford was that others were now following Dexter's lead, and in ever more extreme style.

Warwickshire had a good side for one-day cricket, positive batsmen such as Bob Barber and John Jameson complemented by miserly seam bowling from Tom Cartwright and Jack Bannister. They were led by M. J. K. Smith, who was about to deputize for Dexter as captain of England and, while having very much his own style of doing that job, had plainly taken lessons from his predecessor where limited-overs cricket was concerned. Warwickshire amassed 294 and then defended it with a far-flung field. Lancashire reacted in such a misguidedly aggrieved way to the tactics that two players, Marner and Clayton, were subsequently sacked for deliberate slow scoring and the captain, Ken Grieves, also lost his job.

The reverberations of this were just being felt when the second cup final day dawned gloriously fine and Lord's once more filled to the brim. For the second time, however, it was a low-scoring final, which was against the intention and spirit of the competition, and this one was one-sided, too. Although Dexter lost the toss and Sussex had to field first for the only time during these two triumphant years, they bowled out Warwickshire for a mere 127. It was over, as a contest, by lunchtime, for Warwickshire were 61 for six and Ian Thomson, that master craftsman of a seam bowler who had, earlier in the year, taken ten for 49 against Warwickshire in a match Sussex contrived to lose by being dismissed for 23, had added four more victims to his tally.

Sussex had no trouble with the trifling target and, fittingly, Dexter and Parks were together as they won by eight wickets with 19 overs unused. Superficially, then, Dexter remained crowned in triumph at county level. Beneath the surface, however, things were not so sweet. The second Gillette victory succeeded in

80

keeping the peace but there were unmistakable signs that Dexter had lost interest in the job he had approached with such vigour and fascination four years earlier. It was transmitting itself in various ways, some heated, most humorous, but to those closest to him, Dexter and cricket were drawing inexorably closer to the end of their relationship.

Chapter Six

John Snow summed it up. Dexter, he said, 'was a big-time player, one who responded to atmosphere, liked action and enjoyed the chase and gamble . . . keen when the action was hot, disinterested when the game was dull'. It explains why Dexter inspired Sussex to their Gillette Cup wins in 1963 and 1964, for he himself was inspired by the nature of the project and its spontaneity. It also explains why he was not, in the conventional sense, an enduringly successful county captain, or even an especially popular one. Indeed, the longer his five years in the job proceeded, the less respect he commanded among the Sussex players. It was not that they did not admire him – everyone admired him – or, with hardly an exception, that they disliked him. The majority simply could not relate to his ways and found it increasingly difficult to respond to a leader who gave every impression of having his mind on loftier matters than a county cricket side and its problems.

Here, again, was the perception of haughtiness which has shadowed Dexter through his days. Here, again, people were taking offence at what they imagined to be arrogance. It was not, as many now realize. Robin Marlar calls it 'a genuine vagueness . . . Ted never wanted to cut people dead. In his own mind, he just didn't know or recognize them. There were also people whose names he could not remember, or confused. That is a legacy of public-school life,' added Marlar, an Old Harrovian himself.

Alan Oakman, who has remained in the game, first as a coach and then in administrative roles with Warwickshire, chuckles when reminded of his years under Dexter at Hove, but it is an affectionate chuckle not a malicious one. 'He was a most unusual captain. He came to it with a lot of enthusiasm and then seemed to lose interest,' he said. 'There were days when he would walk into the dressing room and chat to you in a most animated and friendly way, and other days when he would walk straight past you as if you were a complete stranger. Bob Willis, during his playing days, strongly reminded me of Ted, because he too was capable of doing this. The reason was the same in both cases – they are not aloof people, they are simply shy.'

Dexter puts it another way. He is aware that he ignores people, because he is told as much, but he enigmatically declines to confirm that it is always accidental. 'There is a streak in me which doesn't suffer fools. I am also aware that I am not a good socializer on other people's terms, and I am conscious of having the blinkers on at times, so that I appear to ignore someone. If that is what people mean by aloof, then they have a point.'

A county captain, however, has broader responsibilities than simply taking the team on the field and changing the bowling at the right time. He has to create a good image for his club – and no one could say Dexter failed in this, for Sussex were regarded as charismatic, colourful and entertaining – and he has to concern himself with the welfare of his players. There were those, at Sussex, who felt that Dexter did not communicate properly, betraying a lack of concern for his team. When Dexter joined the club, quite the opposite was true, for in Hubert Doggart and David Sheppard, now the Bishop of Liverpool, Sussex had two much-loved characters whose stock-in-trade was conversation, concern and communication. Both, now, had retired and Dexter was left to preside over an increasingly professional age which left some players feeling insecure. The consensus is that he did little to help.

One Sussex player, capped in the early 1960s, regularly complained that Dexter never spoke to him, other than to issue a command on the field or to tell him his batting position. And he was upset by it, believing it to be a slight, almost a sneer. There were others who felt their captain should be spending more of his social time with them, in the bars and steakhouses that they habitually frequented on away trips, rather than in his own circle of friends. And there were those, more than a few of them, whose opinion of Dexter's on-field captaincy declined with the years. No one disputed that he had been a visionary in the Gillette Cup and that, without him, Sussex would probably still have won nothing. But in the six-days-a-week championship circuit that dominated each season, the requirement was more for constant care and attention than occasional shafts of inspiration, and by his own admission Dexter was not best suited to that.

Life was tugging him in a variety of directions, far from all of them connected with cricket, and the commitment demanded by the nature of county cricket was beginning to stir a restless resentment within him. At first it had been fun to commute from the marital flat to Hove, first in his Anglia, then a Borgward and finally, his pride and joy, the pale blue Jaguar, arriving at 10.40 a.m. for a cup of tea, a chat and a look at the pitch (there was not so much physical preparation in those days) before play. Now, it was beginning to intrude upon things he might rather be doing and it was perhaps only because he was captain of England, and obviously needed to play some county cricket between Test match engagements, that his career extended beyond his thirtieth birthday.

There were, however, seasons in the early 1960s when Sussex followers began to believe that the 140-year wait for a championship title might be about to end under Dexter. Often, they would play the most adventurous and invigorating cricket, risking defeat in an attempt to win. More than once, they were still in the running as the final few weeks of the schedule began, but they could never quite carry through the challenge, for they lacked the experience of winning and, probably, the depth of ability within the club. Much to Dexter's regret, for instance, they had no match-winning spin bowler now that Marlar's day was done, and it was this shortcoming, more than any other, which restricted them when the late-summer pitches became dry and conducive to turn.

84

Batting was never a problem in those years, for apart from Dexter and Parks, who would decorate what games they were able to play with some of the finest strokeplay seen in the county game, there was the perennially prolific Ken Suttle. Seam bowling was another notable strength, for the new ball was passed unquestioningly to Ian Thomson, Staffordshire-born and with an unprepossessing action yet, scandalously, thirty-five years old and past 100 wickets in a season for the twelfth consecutive year before he won his first England cap in the winter of 1964–5.

Perhaps the catalyst for his belated recognition was that he took 10 wickets in an innings in a championship match during 1964. It was to be the last time the feat was performed in the county championship until Richard Johnson, a similar stamp of bowler but at the outset rather than in the autumn of his career, took 10 for 45 for Middlesex in 1994. Thomson's instance was peculiarized in that he finished on the losing side, for it occurred on such a rogue pitch at Worthing that two things resulted: Sussex were dismissed in their second innings for 23, in just 55 minutes, and the Worthing ground was struck off the first-class register for the following season. Dexter was away on England duty for that game but he was in charge, on another outground at Hastings a month later, for an interesting flashpoint that has lingered in the memory of John Snow.

After finishing his course at teacher-training college (a fall-back he was destined never to need) and having any ideas of playing as an amateur abandoned for him by the legislation, Snow was creating quite an impression in his first full season of county cricket. He was only twenty-two, and patently raw, but that lithe, long-limbed approach and the whippy, side-on delivery were already attracting compliments. Although he was later to increase his pace, he was bowling quickly enough to have earned the new ball ahead of Tony Buss and, on a rain-affected pitch at Hastings, he threatened to be quite a handful for the Northamptonshire batsmen.

Opening the innings for Northants was the imposing figure of Colin Milburn, whose liking for the hook stroke was well known, and although the conditions indicated a need to pitch the ball up and let the dampness do the rest, Snow was of a mind to take him on. Dexter, unaware of this, had set a ring of close fielders on the leg-side, of whom he was one, and when Snow tried the short ball and Milburn rocked back to hook it for four, the captain's anger was both visible and audible. 'Once he had picked himself up he shouted at me down the pitch,' recalls Snow. 'It wasn't very complimentary and it was a pretty clear instruction to pitch it up. I decided to ignore him, not least, I suppose, because I hadn't taken too kindly to being yelled at like that. Two balls later I dug another one in short. 'Ollie' went for the hook again but found it was too quick and too steep for him. He ended up fending it off his chest and Ted took a very easy catch at leg-slip. He said nothing but I couldn't resist it. I walked down the pitch and said: 'All right, captain, is that how you wanted it pitched up?' That established our positions very clearly and very early in my career and I don't recall ever having a cross word with Ted again. In many ways, you see, we were alike.'

One striking similarity between them was the need for something more stimulating than the average county season offered. Later in his career, Snow achieved a reputation for conserving energy between Test matches and was seldom the same bowler for Sussex that he was for England. Dexter, so it is related by those in the dressing room at the time, revealed his waning interest in county affairs by missing the occasional match. 'There would be a phone call from him on Tuesday afternoon, just as a Test match was ending,' said one team-mate. 'He would say his knee was causing him trouble – as it often did, to be fair – and that he hoped to see us at the weekend.' Dexter was never the hands-on county captain, attending and watching every ball even when not playing. In fact, he was not always watching when he was in the side . . . or not watching the cricket, anyway.

Horse-racing was by now a great diversion for him. Some would have called it a distraction. It was not just the punting, though Dexter was never shy of a bet: the sport itself, its people and its horses, now fascinated him and it was not long before he dabbled, with no great fortune, in racehorse ownership. Televised racing was a salvation to him on afternoons when Sussex were batting or, perhaps, the weather had closed in. He carried his own portable television from game to game and would set it up in a corner of the dressing room, his racing paper and even form-books alongside. 'The reception wasn't always very good,' remembers Alan Oakman, 'and Ted would get the twelfth man to walk around with the aerial until he had a decent picture.' One day at Portsmouth, none of the contortions performed by the twelfth man could produce a watchable screen so Dexter, anxiously awaiting the outcome of his first investment of the afternoon, grabbed the aerial. He discovered that both set and aerial had to be moved into one particular corner of the changing quarters at the United Services ground. It was in the loo and, quite unabashed, he set up shop there for the remainder of the transmission.

Possibly the best-known tale of Ted's fascination with horse-racing concerns a drinks interval on Derby day. I had heard it so often I had begun to believe it apocryphal. Those who were there swear it is true. Dexter had spotted that the Derby off-time roughly coincided with the mid-afternoon drinks break and as, to his chagrin, Sussex were in the field, he concocted a splendid subterfuge. The Sussex twelfth man (who seems, in those days, to have resembled Dexter's fag at Radley) was told to secrete a portable radio on the drinks tray and to ensure that he was on the field promptly. Dexter and his players duly gathered around, anticipating the 'off', but the race had been delayed by a slipped saddle (or maybe a spread plate – different players tell it different ways). With Dexter refusing to accept defeat, a new record was established for the length of a drinks break on an English county ground. If that would appear to some to be taking a liberty, the view would be of little account to Dexter. As John Snow recounts: 'He had his interests and followed them, never worrying about what other people thought. His independence never concerned me at all, possibly because I was a similar type, but I know it upset certain others, in the side and on the committee.'

Perhaps Dexter's ultimate achievement in the arena of mixing business with pleasure was to attend a race meeting while a game was in progress. But any prospect of the Sussex club taking action on what would now be considered an arrant breach of discipline was stymied on the starting-line, as Ted had been invited to play truant by none other than the Duke of Norfolk, president of the club. 'We were batting on the final day of a championship match when the Duke put his head into the dressing room and asked Ted if he'd like to pop up to Brighton races with him,' recalls Alan Oakman. 'Ted needed no persuasion. The trouble was that a declaration was due in mid-afternoon and Jim Parks had to telephone the racecourse to consult Ted about the timing of it. It is the sort of thing that wouldn't happen nowadays and would never have been permitted even then by a club like Yorkshire.'

But Sussex was not a club like Yorkshire. Even the impetus that came from success in the Gillette Cup created nothing in the way of revolution because here was a club deep in tradition and conservatism. Dexter might have achieved more had he played within Yorkshire's regime of constant expectation but he might also have found that the demand for a single-minded approach to cricket drove him into retirement at a still earlier age. At Sussex, and as captain, Ted was allowed his indulgences, one of which was to arrange his travelling schedule around his other sporting interests. Sometimes, this would be a round of golf but often it was a race meeting – either horses or greyhounds, in which Dexter was also pursuing an increasing interest. He was a regular at the Brighton dog-track during home games and his *Sporting Life* usually pointed him in the direction of an evening meeting convenient for each away game. 'Quite a few of us would go along,' explains Snow, 'but Ted was always in charge. He even went to the dogs the night before the Gillette final!'

Sussex, like most counties, travelled to away games in private cars rather than by coach and Dexter invariably took the side's spin bowler, Ronnie Bell, as his passenger. 'Ronnie would do as he was told,' chuckles Oakman, 'and his role was essentially to hold Ted's binoculars and ensure they were going the right way for the races. Many is the time when they arrived at the team hotel at midnight, Ted flushed with the success and excitement of an evening's punting and Ronnie just looking tired and fed-up.'

Oakman cites anecdotes like this in support of his theory that Dexter would have been happier without the burdens of leadership. 'He would have been better playing his county cricket under someone like Peter May or David Sheppard, simply getting on with his own game without the expectation that he should concern himself with other people's problems. For all his presence, as a cricketer and a person, it always struck me that he wanted to be in the background all the time. I remember him sitting an insurance exam, because it was still vaguely thought that he might go into his father's business. He hadn't wanted to take the exam and he certainly didn't want to pass it, because the next logical step was that he would have to go out and sell policies. Ted always preferred people to come to him.'

This unexpected diffidence was mirrored in his captaincy methods. Snow confirms: 'If you were the sort who needed a captain to mother you, Ted was not the right guy. We had very few team talks and those we did have were short and sweet. Some players felt rebuffed when Ted didn't talk to them on a personal basis, but that was just his way. He never was hard, or cold, as he was sometimes made out to be. He just floats along in his own world and, if he ignores you, it is probably because he is deep in thought about something else.' Through it all, Dexter remained a formidable player when mood and circumstances coincided. Sussex's reward for winning the inaugural Gillette Cup was a challenge match, played under the same rules, against the touring West Indies side. It was good for prestige and undoubtedly good for the club's accounts – even better all round when Sussex won the game in some style. The memory of the day, for many of the 15,000 who were there, was the duel between Wes Hall and Dexter. The great fast bowler, an impressive sight to all but the batsman as he hurtled down the Hove slope, gold chain billowing at his neek, had helped West Indies win the Test series 3–1 and he was holding nothing back now against a familiar foe. John

Snow relates: 'Wes was flat out, and that was as quick as anybody in the world, but Ted hit him straight back over his head and the ball clattered into the sightscreen at the top of the ground before anyone had moved. It is the only time in my life I have seen a ball bowled so fast, and hit so hard, that I did not see it in either direction.'

Snow was also in the side when John Price, of Middlesex and England, decided he had Dexter's measure. 'Sport' Price was among the quickest bowlers in the country at the time and he believed that Dexter's weakness was the hook shot. He had made his intentions plain in the first innings of the game, in which Dexter scored only a few, and the contest to be resumed in the second innings was keenly awaited by players of both teams. 'There were no chest protectors around in those days,' explains Snow, 'but Ted fixed a couple of thigh pads across his chest before he went out to bat. Then he proceeded to hook Sport out of the attack.'

Dexter's own theories were sometimes subject to equally spectacular failure. As a batsman (as distinct from as a captain) he had an impatient disregard for the niggling, line-and-length seam bowlers so prevalent in England. Of their type, Derek Shackleton was the master. He took 100 wickets in a season on twenty-two occasions and his career, which began long before Dexter's, was still continuing four years after Dexter's had ended. Perhaps it was this longevity, this self-satisfaction with a metronomic efficiency which carried him through to the age of forty-five, that infuriated the fidget within Dexter. Whatever, he took it into his head that batsmen were unnecessarily inhibited by this 'ordinary' medium-pace bowler and decided to demonstrate this when Sussex met Shackleton's Hampshire at Southampton. 'Ted's theory was that you had to hit him over the top, meeting the ball on the up,' recalls Snow. 'He was caught at mid-on in the first innings and mid-off in the second, while Shack took eight wickets in the match.'

At times, however, he could elevate batting on to a plane accessible to nobody else. These occasions were not confined to Test cricket, either, for Oakman recalls watching in awe from the non-striker's end as Dexter savaged the Surrey attack at the Oval in 1962. 'It was a low-scoring game on quite a difficult pitch, yet Ted smashed Peter Loader around for a couple of hours and made 94, then got out as if the prospect of a century never even entered his head. I still remember Peter May, who was captaining Surrey, walking across to me as Ted went off and saying: "At least the rest of us can get on with the game, now."'

'Getting on with the game' was always a prime motivation to Dexter and accounts for the eccentricity of some of his captaincy. There were days when he would personally allow a game to drift while he vacantly practised golf swings in the outfield (Peter Parfitt, and England team-mate, once famously asked Dexter as they left the ground after a day in the field: 'How many did you go round in today, skipper?') but others when he would react to a stale passage of play with the unorthodox, if not the outrageous. 'Sometimes he would bring on a bowler for all the wrong reasons,' argued Snow. 'Possibly it was because he was just plain bored with what was going on, because Ted had a very low boredom threshold in county cricket. I was personally never sure when I would be asked to bowl and when I would be taken off but if one of Ted's changes brought a wicket it was invariably hailed as a piece of brilliant, inspired leadership.'

One such instance, in which the praise was perhaps deserved, occurred at Chesterfield in May 1964. Sussex's match against Derbyshire was edging towards stalemate on the final afternoon when the home side, 43 behind on first innings, lost two early second-innings wickets to Tony Buss. A stand between the opener, Ian Hall, and the captain, Charlie Lee, then frustrated Sussex and Dexter's solution was to summon Jim Parks to bowl some leg-spin. Now, Parks was not the worst leg-spinner and had at one stage hinted at a future in that direction. But, largely through the insistence and support of Dexter, he had become not only the county wicketkeeper but the England 'keeper, too. No matter. Dexter instructed him to take off his pads and, upon Parks asking who would take over behind the stumps, announced that he had kept wicket at prep school and would do the job himself. So 'Lord Ted', who had indeed done a spot of wicketkeeping, though none since the age of twelve, donned pads and gloves while Parks tried to recall the art of wrist-spin. Typically, it worked, though not in the way that either man had planned. 'Jim bowled a waist-high full-toss,' says Alan Oakman, 'and Charlie Lee missed it and was bowled.'

Dexter would have enjoyed that. It fascinated him to stray from the prescribed routes of cricket matches and occasionally, of course, he ended up in a ditch through his daring. It was, as all who played under him agree, seldom less than interesting when Dexter was in charge and even those who resented his remoteness and became infuriated by his tactics consider that he had rare foresight.

As long ago as 1965, the year in which he took his official leave of the game, Dexter was saying: 'My ideal programme [for the county championship] would be 16 four-day games. The cricketers would come fresh and keen to every one. The present county game as a nursery for Test players is really no good at all. Such a revolution would increase the watching cost per day to members but at least they would be paying for the most lasting ingredient of all products – quality.' It was a little over twenty-five years later that the game came round to Dexter's way of thinking, to what is now generally agreed as the common good, and the step was only taken, even then, because Dexter himself was there to push everyone across the threshold.

Chapter Seven

Between the springs of 1961 and 1963, Ted Dexter played twenty-five times for England. He never missed a Test match and so memorably imposed his batting power upon the game that Richie Benaud calls him 'one of only two great English batsmen since the war', the other being Peter May. But Dexter also became captain of England and at that rarefied level, just as much as on the shop floor of Hove, it was an appointment of mixed blessings. Responsibility had no adverse effect on his batting, quite the opposite if anything, but it also had none on his personality. He continued to appear distant and detached in his personal dealings and, depending on one's viewpoint, either unconventional or eccentric in his tactics. A general view on his time as captain, from those who played under him, would not be complimentary though it remains the story of his life that he infuriated but seldom offended, and was much misunderstood but hardly ever disliked.

Ten of the Test matches during that two-year period were against Australia. It is fair to say that Australians had a jaundiced view of Dexter, whom they regarded as a reasonable image of Douglas Jardine in background, bearing and general arrogance, but that they maintained a healthy respect for his ability. Equally, Dexter identified the Australians as the team he most wanted to beat and the incentive created the ingredients for some of the most stirring deeds of his career. Two such days occurred during summer 1961 and the galling fact that neither was in a winning cause lived uncomfortably with Dexter until two winters later he was able, to some degree, to put matters right. Benaud's team was on a high when it arrived in England in 1961, having just beaten West Indies 2–1 in a thrillingly fought series at home. There had been no overseas tour for England that winter and the hiatus seemed to have done them no good whatever when they conceded a first-innings lead of 321 in the opening Test at Edgbaston. When the final day began, England's second innings stood at 106 for one, the potential for defeat still strong, but Raman Subba Row then completed a century, on his first appearance against Australia, and Dexter batted almost through the day for 180 before, typically, with the match saved, he was out stumped.

Australia won the second Test by five wickets despite being deprived of Benaud due to a damaged shoulder, just about the worst thing that can happen to a leg-spinner. At Headingley, two weeks later, it was the turn of England to be incommoded by injury to a key bowler. Brian Statham was the missing man and it led to a curious selection – though, to many in the game, the real curiosity was why the man concerned had been so neglected down the years. Les Jackson, Derbyshire seam bowler of archetypal coal-mining stock, was now forty and had played his only previous Test match twelve years earlier. He was a bowler of strength, stamina and a skill so rare that Dexter rated him 'the best bowler I ever faced'. Recalling a torture Jackson had administered at Derby, Dexter added: 'No two balls did the same thing and hardly a straight one was bowled.' Jackson took four wickets in this one-match comeback and never again played for England. He featured, however, in a three-day victory, largely brought about by Fred Trueman's 11 wickets, including one spell of 5 for nought.

So it was all-square going into the fourth Test, England cosseting dreams of winning back the Ashes and banishing the sour memories of that 4–0 defeat two years earlier. Those dreams flared into life when Australia were dismissed for 190, the restored Statham taking five wickets. A first-innings lead of 177 was hard currency in this tough-bargaining series and, when the ninth Australian second-innings wicket fell at 334, only 157 ahead, Manchester prepared to acclaim a famous victory. Instead, Alan

Davidson and Graham McKenzie put on 98, leaving England less than four hours to score 256.

It was a stern target, one that some modern Test teams might not even have attempted, but Ted Dexter seldom played his cricket without ambition and, now, he played such an astoundingly good innings that England attained a winning position from which, paradoxically, they lost the match. Coming in when the first wicket fell at 40, Dexter struck 76 in 84 minutes. At the height of his onslaught, Richie Benaud asked for a drinks break. As the weather in Manchester was true to its legend that day, it seemed barely justified but Benaud now confesses that he acted in the same way that a basketball coach does when calling 'time out' if his team is under pressure. 'The scenario', he explains, 'was that McKenzie and Davidson gave us a lifeline and Dexter took it away with one of the best short innings I have ever seen played. I called for drinks, on what was a cloudy, cool Old Trafford afternoon not because we were thirsty but because I wanted a break to regroup. I had a very quick team meeting in the centre of the ground to tell them that, thanks to Ted, there was no way we could now draw the game, it was a case of win or lose.'

Benaud decided to bowl round the wicket – 'almost unheard of for a leg-spinner in those days' – and exploit the leg-stump rough caused, predominantly, by Trueman's follow-through. In 25 balls, he took five for 12, snatching back a match that Dexter's brilliance looked to have decided. It was wonderful bowling and sharp thinking from a master of his craft, and it was only much later that Benaud revealed his damaged shoulder had still been troubling him during his match-winning spell. 'Throughout the match, before each session and during every break in the dressing-room, I had exercise treatment from Dr Alan Bass, the Arsenal doctor, who had travelled to Manchester expressly for the purpose. It involved me pushing my bowling arm and shoulder against great opposite pressure exerted by a physio.'

It became known as 'Benaud's match', yet it might so easily have been Dexter's. Some – England players among them – later expressed the view that the game would not have been lost if

Dexter had not played so well, a perverse logic that Benaud dismisses out of hand. 'It's rubbish. England lost that day because no one else was capable of playing as good an innings as Ted. Ted won the game for them and we grabbed it back by pulling off one of the biggest gambles of all time. We were also lucky – but it was a case of making our own luck. That innings of Ted's, and his other performances that summer, showed us that he was one of the great batting figures to emerge in English cricket.'

But the Ashes were now out of reach again and, when England could only draw at the Oval, the series was lost, too. This game marked the retirement, at thirty-one, of Peter May. He had captained England a record 41 times and his resignation had given the selectors a sensitive decision to make. A winter tour to India and Pakistan loomed, its itinerary so complex and elongated that several senior players, Colin Cowdrey among them, were pointedly unavailable. But Dexter, who had set himself to complete a circuit of the Test-playing countries, was keen to go, which he did as captain.

Trueman, Statham and Lock were numbered among the other luminaries who did not make the trip and the following year's *Wisden* was scathing of the practice: 'The business of leading players declining certain tours needs consideration by the authorities,' thundered Leslie Smith in his tour review.

India rightly point out that they have never seen a full-strength MCC side and resent the fact that the star players make a habit of turning down the trip. Admittedly, English players find the tour harder and less comfortable than any other, but this scarcely justifies players, once they are established, picking and choosing which tour they want to make. It is no secret that in general the men who go to India, Pakistan and Ceylon regard themselves as a 'second eleven', often play like it and are caustic about the stars who stay at home.

Despite this passionate censure, the tactical 'resting' from the less appealing of tours continued for some years, perhaps up to the time that Kerry Packer's advent changed the game for ever. In the early 1960s, however, it was prevalent and seven new Test caps had to be awarded during Dexter's first tour in charge. It was, as *Wisden* affirmed, 'one of the most strenuous tours undertaken by any side'. Stretching across almost five months, the cricket began in Pakistan in October 1961, crossed to India for five Tests and then returned to Pakistan for two more, ending up, just when everyone had had quite enough, with three games in what was then Ceylon.

It was a test of character as much as anything, for many of the party were inexperienced travellers and venues such as Nagpur, Jullundur and Cuttack were far from luxurious – even when I first visited them sixteen years later. *Wisden* said: 'The English players never did accustom themselves to the different type of food, the all-too-many functions and the unusual living conditions, but in the main they were a cheerful set of players.' M. J. K. Smith, who was Ted's vice-captain, adds: 'The attitude to the off-field problems of sickness among players was one of acceptance. You knew you would be ill at some stage and you got through it as best you could. With the heat and enervation, these were hard places to play and whoever was captaining the side had to put on to bowl whoever was capable.'

Maybe Trueman and company had it right. Five-star luxury this was not, and yet for all concerned it was a voyage of discovery. Cricket on the subcontinent had grown remarkably in popularity and almost 2 million people watched Dexter's team play, 1.2 million attending the eight Test matches. And for Dexter, it was a trip that lived with him. The poverty he encountered, especially during the upcountry visits in both India and Pakistan, had a profound effect upon him and was to some degree influential in his adoption of the Church as an important part of life.

As far as the cricket was concerned, Dexter suffered grievously with the spin of the coin. The gambling man in him must have writhed with injustice as he won the toss only once in the eight Tests. Seven times, England were consigned to the field on surfaces that blithely mocked all forms of bowling. India's lowest first-innings score was 380 and, enabled to dictate the pattern of successive games, they wore England down and won the last two Tests to take the series.

The disjointed three-match rubber against Pakistan was won on the strength of victory in the first match during October. It was a close-fought game and when England, needing 208 in 250 minutes for victory, lost their fifth wicket at 108, Pakistan were marginal favourites. But Dexter and Bob Barber won the match with an unbeaten stand at better than a run a minute, so Ted's first game as England captain was a personal triumph. It was, however, the only Test victory he was to taste on that tour, though in Karachi, almost four months later, he produced a herculean all-round effort to ensure the series win.

England went into the match with only three seam bowlers, of whom Dexter was one, and calamity struck when 'Butch' White pulled a muscle in his third over and could not bowl again in the match. Ted was obliged to bowl 18.2 overs in the first innings and then batted almost throughout the England reply, occupying the crease more than eight hours in scoring his first and only double century in Test cricket. It was a monumental innings, the unarguable answer to any who still believed him capable only of dashing cameos, and although it must inevitably have left him fatigued and dehydrated, he proceeded to set a stirring example to his men by taking the new ball, bowling 32 overs and picking up three wickets. There were many occasions in his career when Dexter flaunted his terrific talent but maybe none on which his character, his will to succeed, were so graphically evident.

Captaincy had not changed him. Time was to prove that nothing could. Mike Smith recalls that Dexter remained remote though, as a singular individual himself, he had no quarrel with his number one on that score. 'It never occurred to me that Ted was not comfortable, not relaxed on his own terms,' said Smith. 'But it is true that he was never very close with anyone in the team. What could have been considered off-handedness I put down to basic shyness but I also tended to approve of it. Loners in sport very often turn out to be strong characters. Going your own way is an admirable thing.'

Not everybody agreed, of course, and Dexter's style of leadership was a regular source of debate when the team returned to England, not least among the selectors, of whom Walter Robins had just become chairman. In what, at the time, was an unusually public pronouncement, Robins told the press, following a selectors' meeting in early April, that no player would be considered for England under his stewardship unless he showed himself prepared to play positive cricket. A series against Pakistan was scheduled for the summer of 1962 but Robins's priority was plain. 'We want a captain – above everything else a leader who must answer every bid or challenge Australia make.' Already he was looking ahead to the following winter and the Ashes contest. And what Robins had to say left nobody in any doubt that Dexter had not made an unanswerable case to continue in the job.

'Our captain has to issue his own challenges,' went on Robins. 'We are absolutely in agreement that we do not want someone who might wait for victory to come but a leader who will take positive steps to achieve that victory. We will tell the captain his object is to win every match as soon as possible . . .' and much more along similar lines. It was a speech of the type Dexter made more than once, thirty years later with the roles reversed, but at the time it confirmed that he had some convincing to do if he wanted to take the team to Australia. And he wanted that, perhaps more than anything in his cricket career.

Having made their keynote speech, the four selectors – Doug Insole, Alec Bedser, Willie Watson and Robins – spent the summer observing their candidates at close quarters. Each of the selectors acted as England team manager for at least one of the five Tests against Pakistan, a hopelessly one-sided series that would have ended 5–0 rather than 4–0 if almost two days' play had not been lost to the weather at Trent Bridge. Interest was focused not on the cricket but on the personalities, those who might do well enough to earn an Ashes tour and, in particular, the trio under review to take charge.

99

The two obvious contenders were Dexter and Cowdrey and it was the intention of Walter Robins and his colleagues to weigh up each of them against Pakistan. It seems a somewhat school-masterly way of going about the issue of judging two men whose credentials ought to have been perfectly familiar and it was, in the event, only partially carried through. Dexter captained the first two Tests, won by an innings and nine wickets respectively, and Cowdrey took over for the third, again won by an innings. Pakistan's resistance was now seen to be so spineless that the experiment might have been thought worthless as a pointer for what was to come in Australia, but Cowdrey, who would probably have kept the job for the fourth Test, was ruled out by illness. Suffering a kidney complaint, he also had to miss the Gentlemen versus Players match at Lord's, identified as a tour trial by the selectors. Cowdrey had been due to captain the Gents, who included Dexter, and this was widely considered a broad hint, but when Dexter took over the matter might have been thought settled but for the growing claim of a third candidate.

David Sheppard had, to all intents and purposes, retired from first-class cricket to take the cloth. Now, a fully fledged reverend, he not only made himself available again for Sussex – though for only a handful of matches – he also threw his hat into the ring for the tour captaincy.

Here was a situation unthinkable today. Sheppard, after all, had not played any Test cricket since 1957 and it was even longer – 1954 – since he had led Sussex to second place in the championship in his sole year as captain. He had been thought an excellent captain, probably everything that Dexter was not, but in the long period since, he had not only been ordained but taken a full-time post as warden of the Mayflower Centre in London. Having made himself available for the Australian tour he was, within the general indecision ruling at the time, thought by some a compelling alternative to the wayward Dexter or the warm but unambitious Cowdrey. Walter Robins spoke highly of Sheppard's qualities, which might easily have won the day, and the bizarre situation developed wherein Sheppard made his occasional county appearances playing under Dexter, while likely to usurp him as England captain.

The decision was taken during the Gentlemen versus Players match. Sheppard's century on the opening day led much of the media down a blind alley. For unbeknown to them, Robins had thought again about the wisdom of dispatching a part-time cricketer, even such a popular and respected man as Sheppard, into battle against the old enemy. Homebound commuters were still absorbing their morning-paper headlines, acclaiming the vicar as England captain, when Dexter was being summoned into the committee room at Lord's to hear something rather more to his advantage.

It was a relief to him, there is no doubt about that. Dexter was never one to betray anxiety, much less to discuss it with all and sundry, but the prolonged scrutiny of him and the other two contenders that emanated from this unnatural public trial had taken its toll. When, eventually, England scored a famous victory in Melbourne, he felt the self-fulfilment of the moment more keenly than anything in his career. 'It was a personal triumph for me,' he related, 'because all through the previous season there had been such conjecture over who would lead the team. The selectors could not make up their minds, but in the end I got the job and I felt that this victory justified the faith that people had had in me.'

This was not, however, destined to be a triumphal march around the Antipodes for Ted Dexter and he emerged from it with as many questions asked about his captaincy as answered. It was a gruelling trip by any standards. The party left England on 27 September and returned six months later, having played 32 matches. Within that tour, Dexter was on show as never before and, perhaps, never again. As a captain of the most glamorous and publicized of all cricket tours, it was not only his cricketing ability that was laid bare but his character, too. And, because he was captain, he was there to be judged.

Chapter Eight

Fred Trueman has never been shy of expressing his views. The chips on his shoulders may seem the size of footballs and the passion of his protests sometimes stronger than their logic, but give Fred something worth complaining about and he will offer a memorable moan. He did not care for the style of the Dexter leadership in Australia and he did not mind who knew as much. 'A lot of tactical mistakes were made – vital ones – and I reckon Ted Dexter must take the blame,' said Trueman, of that long and grimly fought tour. 'I liked the man a lot and he could bat beautifully but he was no captain of England. He had more theory than Darwin, but little practical experience to back it up.'

It was not simply the captain's tactics which offended Trueman. He found himself at odds with the hierarchy of the party and their chosen way of conducting the trip, which is, perhaps, not to be wondered at. The Gentlemen and Players distinction had officially been buried but the social chasms still yawned. Trueman was playing under Oxbridge captain and vice-captain (Cowdrey), with a vicar (Sheppard) as senior player, and an Earl Marshal of England, the Duke of Norfolk, as tour manager. This met with Dexter's quiet accord – the Duke, after all, was president of his county and a racegoing chum – but to others it was unfathomable. Alan Ross, chronicling the tour in his book *Australia '63*, wrote that the appointment 'was as surprising at the outset as if Mr Macmillan had suddenly volunteered for the job to escape the Opposition battering over the Common Market and to avoid an English winter'. Predictably, Trueman's reaction was indignant. Transport him to his commentary-box mode and he would doubtless have growled: 'Ah joost don't know what's going off out there.' But when the Duke's racing interests coincided with the ecclesiastical pursuits of David Sheppard and the magnetic arrival of Dexter's wife, Trueman could contain himself no longer: 'All that the newspapers and television programmes were full of was where the Duke's horses were running, where David Sheppard was preaching and what Mrs Dexter was wearing. I became extremely fed up with this, reasoning that we had come to Australia to play cricket, so I was frank when a newspaperman asked me what I thought of the tour up to then. I told him I was a bit confused, not knowing whether we were supposed to be playing under Jockey Club rules, for Dexter Enterprises or engaged on a missionary hunt.'

Trueman, of course, craved attention for himself, and that he was receiving so little due to the charisma of Dexter, the Duke and the dog-collar might have contributed to his feelings as much as any altruistic desire for the all-for-one spirit. He was not, however, alone in his resentment, and when Susan Dexter landed in Australia prior to the second Test, relations between her husband and the cricket press were soon put on a confrontational level. Susan had not come out entirely for a holiday and neither was it claimed that she had. Ted had sought, and received, permission from MCC for his wife to join the party earlier than was customary and to engage in some modelling work which, on occasions, included Dexter. Among those who regarded this as unseemly was the former Australian all-rounder Keith Miller. Under the provocative and slightly imaginative headline 'Cricket Row Over Susan' – there was no 'row' except that argued by the media – Miller condemned the Dexter modelling assignments for 'turning the England captaincy into a commercial gimmick'.

It may mischievously be construed that Miller was betraying jealousy: in his day he had been the Dexter of Australia, a larger-than-life sportsman who hit the ball ferociously hard, bowled fast and lived life to the full. He had the common touch, too, which always eluded Dexter, many of his virtues and some of his vices. They shared, and still do, a passion for gambling. But Miller played in an age when the commercial rewards were few; so too, compared to today's cricketers, did Dexter, but by so freely flaunting one avenue that he had opened up, he might have stirred ill feeling among those who would have enjoyed such a chance. Whatever Miller's motive for the piece – and perhaps it was nothing more sinister than a demanding editor with a fixed idea in his head – Dexter was furious, not least when the subsequent saga of follow-up stories made life uncomfortable for Susan. 'A fortnight after arriving in Australia,' he recalled later, 'she was in tears, protesting that she should never have come and that she ought to go home.'

Trueman's indignation had been fired long before then, however – on the journey out, in fact. To avoid making a long tour even longer, the party had flown as far as Aden, then boarded *Canberra* for the remainder of the journey to the Western Australia port of Fremantle. On the ship, Dexter encountered the athlete Gordon Pirie, and was much taken by his theories on the sedentary lifestyle cricketers enjoyed at such times. He invited Pirie to conduct some exercise classes on deck, much to the horror of certain players, and also encouraged him to advise on diets. This was too much for Trueman. 'He came to me and said I should stop eating steaks and go on a diet of nuts and lettuce like him,' exploded Trueman. 'He also said he knew a man who always ate food like that and was still chasing reindeer round the Arctic at the age of ninety-five. I told him I had no intention of chasing reindeers at any age, only Australians, and I needed steaks to do that . . . Ted Dexter was still very taken by the man and tried to insist on the team following Pirie's instructions. But I concluded my final session with him by expressing the hope that he could swim, because if he kept bothering me he had every chance of going over the side.'

An amusing diversion, but it indicates how Dexter's captaincy was inevitably influenced by transient theory and how this was bound to bring him into conflict with the earthier professionals of his team. He was aware of this, though perhaps oblivious to resentment caused by his social éliteness. As a figure of rare glamour, in contemporary cricket, Dexter was the subject of attention wherever he went and, while he could, and did, do nothing to prevent this, he was also thought by some to have done little to promote a team togetherness that might have shifted the spotlight off his personal star.

His social leanings were certainly more to champagne than beer, more to the Duke of Norfolk and the racecourse than to Alec Bedser and the hotel bar. Bedser was assistant manager of the tour, his solid, unfussy manner forming an effective foil to the aristocratic air of the manager and captain. Alec's habitual lair was the bar and he could always be bearded there by players with a worry or a grievance. Not that they all had grievances against the captain. Far from it. A. C. Smith, now the chief executive of the Test and County Cricket Board but then an ungainly but effective twenty-five-year-old wicketkeeper with Warwickshire, recalls: 'The beer drinkers on that tour were Alec, Brian Statham and myself. There was no good wine in Australia in those days and we came to like the petrol-pump style of refill at Australian bars. Other players would join us over our nightly beer but we never saw Ted at the bar. I don't think any of us considered him aloof for it, though. It was just accepted that he did things differently.'

Smith had much for which to thank Dexter during those months, because against all prior expectations he was chosen for the Test team ahead of John Murray, the stylist from Middlesex. The preference for Smith was thought to be entirely Dexter's initiative, though Smith claims no knowledge of this. What he does say, revealingly, is that the faith inspired him. 'I don't know if it was Ted alone who stood out for me but in two Test matches on that tour I kept wicket better than I had ever done.' Indeed, Smith believes Dexter was unfairly maligned as a captain. 'He was a much better England captain than he was given credit for. He could *look* blank at times but there was always something going on in his head. He had, and still has, a restlessly active mind. I could not understand why a few senior players took against him.'

Alan Ross attempted to quantify this in his book:

He [Dexter] had his faults, certainly, but in the main these lay in the handling of his own players and they did not demonstrably affect the results of the Tests. He spent little time with his team off the field but he was not alone in this. Jardine, Hammond, Hutton were equally remote characters, and similar complaints, one recalls, were constantly levelled at May . . . It would seem that the price of cricketing pre-eminence, added to a captain's strains and responsibilities, is a kind of withdrawn aloofness that is not entirely inseparable from the single-mindedness essential to the great player . . . Social responsiveness, affability, evenness of mood are not noticeably part of Dexter's personality, though he is consistent to the extent that he would as unconcernedly cut the Duke of Norfolk or the chairman of the selectors as he would look through a plain hostess at a cocktail party. Where he failed in his relations with his team was that he left them overmuch to their own devices, often without guidance or consideration, when both would have been appreciated.

Another journalist on the tour was John Woodcock, for many years my predecessor as cricket correspondent of *The Times*. There have been few shrewder, more discerning observers of character on the cricket circuit than Woodcock, and his judgement is that Dexter was undoubtedly shy, often bloody-minded and sometimes even naïve. 'In a curious way, he could be unworldly,' says Woodcock. 'He didn't react to things in the normal way. He had great strength of character and a lot of people held him in awe but, as a captain, he took very little advice about anything and he would do some very odd things while apparently being oblivious to people's reactions.'

Woodcock recalls how, in the build-up to the Test series on that tour, Dexter absented himself in a most unconventional way. 'The team had played very badly in the last fixture in Perth and lost by ten wickets to a Combined XI. The next game was in Adelaide against South Australia and Ted just was not seen. He played golf and then went to Melbourne to watch the Melbourne

Cup race meeting. Many people on the tour were amazed but Ted could see nothing wrong. It was typical of him that in the next match he made a wonderful hundred before lunch.'

That century, against a strong Australian XI captained by Neil Harvey, contained a stroke that has lodged in many memories. It was a straight six against the Test off-spinner Tom Veivers, hit flat and phenomenally hard. Raymond Illingworth, England's senior off-spinner on tour, recalls it with admiration: 'It must have carried some 150 yards,' he said. 'A fantastic shot which only Ted could have produced. He could strike a ball harder than anyone I have ever seen.' Woodcock relates that Dexter played another astonishing stroke during the tour, clearing the grandstand at Adelaide and landing in the tennis courts – where Test match lunch parties last all day. These fleeting memories are merely indicative of a general impression; whatever the reservations many expressed about Dexter the captain, none doubted that in 1963 Dexter the batsman was an awesomely impressive figure. *Wisden*'s account of the tour describes how 'a thrill went round every ground when he strode majestically to the wicket, and most bowlers feared the punishment they were about to receive'. He did not make a century in the Tests but his 481 runs were a record for an England captain in Australia. The responsibilities, then, did not shackle his batting talent.

One of the many contradictions about Dexter, however, was that while his batting conjures vivid memories of flair and adventure, his captaincy, especially at Test level, was widely criticized for being rigid, unimaginative and plain negative. This was not what was promised during the early days of this tour in the Australian spring of late 1962. Both Dexter and the Duke of Norfolk were faced by endless questioning from an avid, curious Australian media, and positive cricket was the theme they invariably preached. But for Dexter, being positive in tactical terms did not necessarily mean being overtly cavalier. He was later to demonstrate his ability to be successful through being mean with his deep-set fields and dependence on seam bowling when leading Sussex in the Gillette Cup. Now, with the greater goal of an Ashes victory as his motivation, theory, as ever, was to the fore. If some chose to interpret his strategies as defensive, Dexter appeared not to care.

Two theories, at least, preoccupied Dexter in the run-up to the first Test but only one of them received much attention. The plot that passed largely unnoticed concerned the use of off-spin. This was still the age when off-spinners were thought an essential part of the game-plan in Australia, and England, perhaps excessively, took three in their squad – Raymond Illingworth, Fred Titmus and David Allen. Dexter was open-minded about which of them he should regard as his senior Test spinner but he was aware that all three shared a common style, attacking the stumps with a field strong on the legside.

Dexter's idea, simple enough in its conception, was that they should alter the habits of a lifetime and concentrate on bowling outside off-stump, encouraging the batsmen to drive against the spin. Illingworth, apprised of the plan, pursued it willingly enough in one match, took a few wickets and emerged with figures that would have flattered him more but for several dropped catches. He was not unimpressed. 'Ted might have introduced a whole new method of bowling off-spinners on hard wickets overseas,' Illingworth related. 'I have often wondered what might have happened if those catches had been taken.' Despite this guarded endorsement from one of his spin trio, however, Dexter had already mentally abandoned the plan. To Illingworth's great surprise, it was never raised again.

The truth behind this was that Dexter had encountered opposition from Allen, a man he liked and respected, and in trying to overcome it and convince him of the tactical merit, he had lost Allen's confidence. Dexter was mortified. 'Here was a man who had learned his trade, who had since proved himself (and did even on that tour under my misguidance) to be as good an off-spinner on hard wickets under the sun as anyone. And here I was trying to tell him his job. Now there is nothing wrong with a captain telling a bowler what to do but if by doing so he loses the bowler's confidence – shatters that mutual understanding where captain trusts bowler's ability and bowler trusts captain's tactical appreciation – then the whole delicate chain is broken. And by insisting for just too long that David Allen should listen to me I broke down that relationship and deprived the side of a great bowler for much of the tour.'

Despite his regret over this backfiring strategy, Dexter is aware that his critics will consider the episode entirely in character. He was always that way, they insist – dabble with a theory, then throw it away and flit on to something new. Brian Statham, for instance, did not feud with Dexter in the style of his great chum and new-ball partner Trueman, but he was no more a fan of his leadership. 'Ted was one captain I never fully understood,' said Statham. 'I don't think anyone else in the dressing room did, either. He did things at times which were difficult to understand. He made moves, and bowling changes, which were completely out of keeping with the run of the game and which sometimes resulted in the opposition wriggling off the hook.' There is something in the harshness of this judgement, too, for it was not in Dexter's nature to play everything by convention. It bored him to be in the field against unadventurous batting, probably because it was so starkly at odds with the way he liked to bat, and it diverted and stimulated him to try the unorthodox.

Hence, his other, better-publicized pre-series tactic, which came to the disapproving attention of the Australian captain, Richie Benaud, and caused a degree of controversy. Summing up the style of his opposite number, in 1993, Benaud remarked: 'Ted was such a natural all-round sportsman that the theory side of things always came as a surprise to me. My own theory is "keep it simple" but Ted at times keeps it complicated. As a captain, I would rate him okay, but not much higher than that. There was often innovation in his captaincy but on that 1962–3 tour he was negative at times, once in the state game against New South Wales. I had heard that in the Australian XI game at Melbourne the previous week there had been some negative field settings and the story I had was that they intended to use "George" Statham slanting in at the pads with a legside field. That happened in Sydney the following week, where my New South Wales side won by an innings and plenty with a day to spare,' added Benaud, modestly failing to mention that this was largely because he destroyed the MCC second innings by taking seven for 18. 'It was in the dressing room on the second evening of that game that I mentioned to one newspaper writer that I might have to revise my ideas on how I would approach the series if Ted persisted with such tactics. After the ensuing publicity, we had no further problems.' So here was Benaud, five years Dexter's senior and vastly more experienced a captain, using the media to trump an experimental tactic. He did it again, to some effect, according to John Woodcock: 'Benaud was the first captain in my knowledge to conduct press conferences at the end of a day's play. Ted was thus expected to do the same but he really didn't cope very well and Benaud was always seen in the better light for it.'

Benaud himself believes that Dexter suffered through the presence of his aristocratic manager. 'I think he was hampered a good deal by the high profile of the manager. The Duke was very pleasant but the captain should be in charge of the team and be seen to be in charge. The media were inclined to push Ted into the background in my own opinion, and I thought it did him a disservice.' He does add, however: 'Ted, unfortunately for him, is rather naïve about the media. He fails to understand that tongue-in-cheek remarks are God's gift to headline writers who have the ability to turn a throwaway line into the equivalent of the *Titanic* in as much time as it takes to raise an eyebrow.' This characteristic cost Dexter dear in his latter days as chairman of the England committee, but it did him no favours in Australia in 1962.

Dexter's best answer to any charge of inadequacy was always his vibrant cricket and, as the Tests loomed, he continued in prime form. At Brisbane, in the final first-class game of the lengthy warm-up schedule, he almost produced an extraordinary win over Queensland. The state side had apparently made the game safe by slowly compiling 433 for seven in their first innings but Dexter's sprightly innings of 80 in even time urged MCC towards a lead of 150 against an attack in which Wes Hall, the great West Indian spending a lucrative season in Australia, was expensively wicket-less. There seemed insufficient time to force a result but Dexter was invariably at his best against such odds. Seizing the ball, he took four wickets for one run, three of them bowled, and Queensland finished gratefully at 94 for seven.

Alan Smith, who was keeping wicket, was an admirer of Dexter's bowling. 'He had a real kick when he was in the mood and I would often be taking the ball head high. The thing was, Ted never saw himself as a 500-overs-a-year man. To him, it was just a diversion, but he was certainly underrated. He could swing the ball both ways and he hit the pitch very hard.' Smith had a more painful memory of that game, because he needed three stitches behind his left ear after ducking into a short ball from Hall. Fortunately for him, the damage was minor and, two days later, Dexter sprang his surprise by naming Smith in the side for his Test début.

It was a drawn game, which England had to chase after losing the toss on a good Gabba pitch. For Dexter, who made a rapid 70 in the first innings and a more measured 99 in the second, it was a satisfactory start. After a few country games, a win over Victoria and a draw in the Christmas fixture against South Australia, in which Colin Cowdrey made 307, the New Year Test in Melbourne began. It provided England with their first win in Australia for two tours and Dexter with the finest memories of his cricketing career.

The context here is all-important. Dexter had not forgotten – could not forget – his personal indignities in Australia four years earlier and that England had lost two consecutive series to the oldest enemy. Beating them was a crusade, and that he should do so in a thrilling match in the vast Melbourne ground, watched by almost a quarter of a million spectators, was immeasurably fulfilling.

Only 15 runs separated the teams on first innings, England replying with 331 to Australia's 316. Dexter and Cowdrey continued in peak form, making 93 and 113 respectively, and when Fred Trueman, responding big-heartedly to his captain, no matter

111

his misgivings about him, took five second-innings wickets, Australia's disappointing 248 gave England a target of 234. A short period remained on the penultimate evening – long enough, however, for Dexter to take his bravest decision of the game. When Geoff Pullar was out with the total only 5, the conventional response would have been to send out a nightwatchman. Dexter considered the option, and instead marched in himself. 'I felt it important, as captain, to show an example,' he explained later. 'I suppose it would have been egg-on-my-face time if I'd got out but you have to show confidence in yourself, even if it means a gamble. The old pros in the side, like Barrington, Graveney and Titmus, probably thought I was wrong, but it enabled me to be in a position to dictate first thing next morning, and that was what I wanted.'

Dexter has always maintained that, in the same position, Australia would have failed to reach that target on the final day. If this is his way of clapping himself on the back, it is doubtless merited, for on this of all days, the power of his personality blended with the innovativeness of his approach and the passion of his desire for victory to create a feeling he has never forgotten. Ted made 52 that day, fairly modest by his own standards, and it was not an innings decorated with flittering boundaries, yet he ranks it as the greatest innings of his life and the sensation that followed victory as the most satisfying that cricket was ever to give him.

For his partner, during the critical first phase of that last day, he had the man who came so close to winning the captaincy, David Sheppard. It had not been a distinguished Test match for 'the Church' up to that point. He was out for nought in the first innings and had dropped two catches. But now, when it mattered most, he rose purposefully to the challenge. Before play, Dexter suggested to him that on this big ground boundaries would be difficult so, to put pressure on the Australians, they should run everything positively, taking all sharp singles available and turning ones into twos and twos into threes. As with all of Dexter's ploys, there was a degree of the gambling instinct behind it and as a quick glance at the dismissals shows that both he and his partner were run out, it could be thought to have backfired. But not a bit of it. 'It worked like a charm,' said Dexter. 'We ran them ragged and, even though we both perished by the sword, we carried out the plan so successfully that it showed everyone what could be done. We demoralized them so much that in the end we won with 75 minutes to spare.'

Sheppard was run out with the scores level but by then he had made 113, the third and last of his Test centuries. Benaud, for once, was powerless and against all expectations England were ahead in the series. It took a while, however, for the result to impress itself on the victorious captain. 'The strange thing is that it did not come to me until we were sitting in the coach outside the ground after the match,' relates Dexter. 'Then it suddenly dawned on me that I was captain of England and we had beaten Australia on their own ground. It was the greatest sense of elation that I ever had in cricket and nothing that happened later took away that moment of triumph.'

Dexter had all too little time to savour it. Within a fortnight, England had been badly beaten in Sydney and the series was once again level. Alan Davidson, that predatory left-arm seam and swing bowler, gave Australia their nemesis, taking four wickets in the first innings and five for 25 as England collapsed miserably to 104 all out in the second. Australia, left needing only 67 for victory, lost but two wickets in the process and so the enervating heroics of New Year in Melbourne had been negated at the first opportunity. It was 1–1 with two to play, but that was how the score was to stay.

It was this anticlimax that so many observers found disappointing. The Tests in Melbourne and Sydney had both, in their individual ways, been dramatic but the two subsequent games not only ended in stalemate but were played, by both teams, with inhibitions that told of a fear of failure. Scapegoats were sought for this perceived short-changing of a once enraptured cricketing public and Dexter, unsurprisingly, was regarded as the natural fall-guy. That role might equally have gone to Benaud, for he had been no less calculating than Dexter in his caution, but the Australian media were already engaged on a crusade to belittle Dexter and they were not about to spurn an opportunity such as this.

What has to be appreciated is that it is only in the past twenty years that British newspapers have upgraded their coverage of Test cricket. In the early 1960s not every newspaper sent a correspondent to a home match, let alone on an overseas tour, and the days of broader, brasher coverage, one journalist writing a match report and another the news or colour story of the day, were still far distant. In Australia, however, this transition had already occurred. Their newspapers employed a professional journalist for their cricket reports and a former Test player for his subsidiary views. Keith Miller was one such, and he seldom sat on the fence of any issue, but many others were also involved in this lucrative adjunct to a cricket career, now increasingly being explored by former England players. Bill O'Reilly and Lindsay Hassett earned great respect for their newspaper columns but others were less esteemed. Neil Harvey, who actually played in the series, was one who wrote especially harshly of Dexter, and, whether or not his views were properly researched and balanced, they inevitably had an influence on those who read them. In his book, *Australia '63*, Alan Ross wrote in his summary of the tour:

> Harvey's articles have earned him some money but they have done him harm quite incommensurate with his fee . . . Harvey may well dislike Dexter; he is at liberty to believe that Dexter does not play the kind of cricket he cares for, but the bald, unsubstantiated terms in which he voiced his disapproval cheapened him, not Dexter.

Dexter tells a story of having dinner with Harvey at the tail-end of the tour. It was a convivial dinner, he recalled, and in the course of a wide-ranging conversation he was under the impression that any old sores had healed to leave something approaching friendship. He was quickly disabused of this notion as, within a matter of days, Harvey's name appeared above the most poisonous of all the articles demeaning Dexter's captaincy of England.

It was Neil Harvey, more than anyone, who ensured that England could not regain the series advantage during the fourth Test in Adelaide. Harvey made 154 in the first innings before, no doubt with particular satisfaction, Dexter dismissed him. But Australia, having won an important toss on a perfect pitch, totalled 393, a platform from which to defend a game they had, throughout, been intent primarily on not losing – hence, the strengthening of their batting order at the expense of their bowling resources. England, with an opening partnership that failed to function, as it had throughout the series, were always chasing the game and, before too long, seemed as satisfied as Australia with the draw. Dexter made the point that in such circumstances the series was the thing, rather than the individual games, but it did not prevent criticism of the unambitious cricket seen during the invariably festive Adelaide week.

There was a hiatus of more than a fortnight before the final, decisive Test match in Sydney and the MCC side spent the time playing a four-day fixture in Melbourne and three minor games in Canberra, Dubbo and Tamworth. At least, they were all scheduled to be minor matches until the Canberra fixture, against the Prime Minister's XI, was accorded inflated status by Sir Donald Bradman's agreement to play his first cricket in fourteen years. This, alone, was sufficient to fill the ground with both spectators and an unrealistic level of anticipation. Bradman, after all, was in his fifty-fifth year and although he had been sufficiently serious in his acceptance to have several net practices in the days prior to the game, it was hardly likely that he would return in his form of twenty years earlier. In some ways, of course, his presence, dominating the occasion, posed a problem for Dexter as captain of the opposition.

Humour was his first haven though, as so often with Dexter, it came through a comment that was open to misinterpretation. As Sir Donald, rapturously received by the packed crowd, reached the middle for his innings, Dexter strolled across to welcome him.

115

'Straight out of Madame Tussaud's,' he said to cricket's most revered old boy, which might have been variously deemed a nicely-judged ice-breaker or gratuitously offensive. What followed, however, was to have the majority, who wanted only to see Bradman at the crease for an hour, tear at their hair in frustration.

Tom Graveney was having a rare bowl at that stage and seemed just about right for the job of giving a fifty-four-year-old a gentle reacquaintance with his bat. But, for reasons best known to himself, Dexter replaced him with his new-ball bowler, Brian Statham. There was nothing Statham desired less than to spoil the party for everyone but it had been the work of a lifetime to groove his length and line and he was not the man to offer easy runs. Bradman was out fifth ball, playing on, and the crowd hushed in shock and dismay.

'He had jammed down too late on a yorker,' recalled John Woodcock, who covered the game for *The Times*. 'To have Statham on against him was extraordinary but Dexter was not being vindictive, merely thoughtless.' Dexter himself understandably saw it differently, believing that Statham, bowling accurately and at well below his normal pace, was the man to enable Bradman to regain a little rhythm in what was inevitably an ungenuine contest. 'Statham bowled him a nice length, all outside off stump,' he explained. 'But the Don covered up and in some perverse way the ball trickled from the inside edge on to his pads, on to the wicket, and the bail fell off. It was almost as bad a moment as when Hollies bowled him for nought in his last Test match at the Oval.'

Justified or not, Dexter had now courted further unpopularity, a situation destined to deteriorate when, at length, the last Test was played. Dexter chose all three of his off-spinners, Illingworth being included as much for his batting as bowling and, having lost patience with the opening pair of Sheppard and Pullar, promoted Cowdrey to go in first. On winning the toss, his game plan revolved around making 350 as an insurance against defeat, then releasing his bevy of spinners on what was reckoned to be an unreliable pitch. But the England first innings never really accelerated out of second gear: they managed only 195 for five on the first day, totalled 321 and conceded a deficit of 28 despite five wickets for Titmus. Although Ken Barrington then added 94 to his first-innings century, England had left themselves too little time to manoeuvre and Dexter's declaration at lunch-time on the final day seemed no more than a gesture. When Australia lost four wickets before tea, the game had been tweaked back to life but the pitch was still too bland, the time too short, the stalemate inevitable, the derision loud and long.

'It was a fiasco,' admitted Dexter, 'both from the watching and, to a large extent, from the playing point of view . . . the whole tour was written off into the bargain. In one game, the whole of a good tour and much fine cricket was cast aside, utterly rejected.' These were bitter words, redolent of the disenchantment Dexter had come to feel for the perceptions of his tour, his team, his captaincy, his character. And it had not quite ended.

'I had my last brush with the press when I said, light-heartedly, that the Ashes were a bane and a nuisance and that if they were abolished and each man paid £1000 for winning there would probably have been a result. This was only to show that cricket was *not* a comedy act, a knockabout turn, that it conformed to certain traditional features and that once you played within these rules and conditions, this was the only game you could expect.' Dexter was aggrieved and surprised when the media chose to interpret his throwaway remark rather differently, accusing him of avarice and linking the remark, in opportunist journalistic style, with the commercial activities they had previously condemned. As ever, some of the criticism was hysterical but even the more measured observers considered Dexter's remark ill-judged. Alan Ross wrote: 'I trust he did not fully understand the implications of what he said; if he did, then he has forfeited every right to go on being England's captain.'

The Melbourne victory, the innings of his life and 'the greatest sense of elation that I ever had in cricket' must have seemed years remote as a chastened, thoughtful and perhaps disillusioned Dexter completed his antipodean adventure with three Tests in New Zealand, all won as convincingly as was to be expected, and returned to England to prepare for a summer series with West Indies. He was to keep the captaincy. He was also to retain the mastery with a bat that elevated him above average Test players and pitched him into compelling confrontations with the best and most hostile bowlers of his generation. In Australia it had been the wiles of Benaud and the probing skills of Davidson. Now, it was the raw, uncomplicated speed of Wes Hall and Charlie Griffith. And, oh, yes, more controversy.

Chapter Nine

Cricket has a great deal for which to remember 1963. Two of its most esteemed knights, Sir Jack Hobbs and Sir Pelham Warner, died that year. Yorkshire won the championship for the fourth time in five summers, and were now without peer as the successors to Surrey in their domination of the county game. Knockout cricket arrived that summer, and so did the West Indies. Between them, they made it a season of drama and theatre for English cricket, which saw hitherto emptying grounds filled to the brim. The game had begun to boom and Ted Dexter was at the fore of almost everything.

Exasperated though he had been by the commonly held opinion that his captaincy in Australia was shallow, if not downright negative, he did not brood overlong on it. He had, after all, scored more Test runs than any previous England captain had managed in Australia and the respect he had commanded from the Australians was in stark, gratifying contrast to their view of him four years earlier. Richie Benaud may have pulled a few strokes, through being a more calculating, manipulative and accomplished captain, but his having been apparently preoccupied with his opposite number was a compliment in itself.

As Alan Ross wrote in *Australia '63*: 'For most of the series Benaud seemed obsessed by Dexter's presence and if his own sparse haul of wickets included Dexter's more often than anyone else's, this was of only personal significance.' Ross believed that the burden of leadership finally bowed Dexter. 'In the end, Dexter had too much to do, the consequence of which was that he lost his attacking flair . . . but in the initial stages, when Benaud wore

119

an aura of invincibility and Davidson threatened to lay waste, it was Dexter, almost contemptuously, who reduced them to human scale.' So, whatever the individual misgivings about his suitability to lead, his man-management skills and his tactical breadth, there was no sensible cause to doubt the influence of his batting. No other Englishman of his generation possessed such a talent for the great innings. He was to play another – in many memories, his greatest – during 1963, and it was to come during a Test match of such twists, sub-plots and constant drama that Dexter later reflected: 'No writer of fiction would have dared to present such a story.'

This, of course, was the Lord's Test, the game that has survived cluttered decades through its compelling images of Dexter's ferocious batting, the bruises decorating Brian Close's torso and the plaster on Colin Cowdrey's broken left arm as he went out through an astonished Long Room to save the match. Ranging against all three of the heroes was fast bowling of a concerted intimidation seldom seen on any ground before. Wesley Hall was in his pomp but so, too, was the man responsible for the ongoing controversy of that summer and several to follow, Charlie Griffith.

Dexter made himself unpopular with Griffith through openly subscribing to the view that he, Griffith, was a chucker. He was not alone in this. Tom Graveney and Ken Barrington also protested about Griffith's action and, in Barrington's case, the issue became so personally stressful that he needed to take a break from the game. Colin Cowdrey says that he was shunned by Griffith for tacitly supporting Graveney's stance. Cowdrey also found the tyres of his Jaguar let down at around this time and the inevitable links were made. But Dexter was England captain and this set him apart. Both men acknowledged this. The views of the captain were more pertinent than those of the rank-and-file, and Dexter did not issue his thoughts without careful consideration. Griffith's degree of distress related as much to the accuser as to the gravity of the charge and he took the most serious exception when Dexter, having pursued private and diplomatic means of having the suspect action investigated, wrote about it in his *Observer* column, late in 1964. West Indies were about to tour Australia and the timing was sensitive, to say the least.

Griffith, who grew up in a poor, God-fearing and happy family amid the sugar plantations at the northern end of Barbados, never wavered in his conviction that the doubts being raised over his action were based upon fear of his devastating yorker. According to Michael Manley in *A History of West Indies Cricket*:

> His reaction is understandable when it is remembered that the complaints were made by the batsmen who had to face him. For example, Ted Dexter had captained England against Griffith in 1963 and made no official complaint. Yet on the eve of the Australian tour of 1964–5 he said in his newspaper column that the results would be meaningless if Griffith were allowed to bowl against them as he had done the summer before. It must be assumed, of course, that Dexter had not considered the worth of his judgement should Australia have won. Griffith can be forgiven for finding it strange that Dexter should have chosen that moment to launch his attack.

The validity of this argument is that Dexter was treading a precarious course between his duties as a distinguished cricketer and his freedom as a well-read columnist. It was not to be the last occasion on which an outspoken view in print was to be held against his cricketing persona, rather than his journalistic one. Manley's reference to the 1963 series, however, is hollow, for although Dexter thought it unwise to go public on his views while the Tests were in progress, he was anything but unconcerned and inactive. As early as the first match of the series, indeed, Dexter was watching a spell from Griffith with Cyril Washbrook, one of the England selectors, and expressed astonishment at the pace generated by some of the deliveries. His suspicions were already aroused.

Dexter's next move was to approach Gubby Allen, the then President of MCC and one of his mentors. He told Allen of his convictions and urged him to take some action before the issue

121

became an international incident. What subsequently occurred in the committee room at Lord's is a matter for speculation but no umpire called Griffith for throwing during the 1963 tour, on which he was undeniably at his best. This situation changed markedly when the West Indians returned three years later and two umpires, Arthur Fagg and Charlie Elliott, took action against him.

In recent years the subject matter of the game's controversies has moved on. Ball tampering is the vogue, or perhaps dissent. Chucking is regarded as *passé*, which is not to say that there is any less of it. In the early 1960s, however, no subject in sport aroused such passions as throwing and the Griffith affair rumbled on, providing a steady stream of back-page headlines, long after this momentous 1963 series had ended. During that summer, however, it was just one of the sub-plots, for the nation was enchanted by a West Indian side which knew how to win, as well as to entertain, and by the influx to so many grounds of their noisy yet good-humoured supporters, mostly emigrants now living in England's inner cities but discovering, in the joyously successful cricket being played by their countrymen, an outlet for their stifled native pride. It produced the sort of scenes no English ground had ever previously encountered and, wondrously, they came unaccompanied by the type of confrontational aggression that would be feared today.

There were four West Indians in *Wisden*'s five Cricketers of the Year, which says much for the impact made by Frank Worrell's side. That it was unexpected can be gauged in various ways. First, the touring team came with no established reputation, for this was a team in its infancy. Deryck Murray, the young wicketkeeper, had never even met Wes Hall until the players assembled in London towards the end of April. And, although much interest had been excited by West Indies' tie in Brisbane in 1960, this was the English public's first sighting of the new force in world cricket. If they required some convincing of their credentials, so, too, did certain England players.

England had lost none of their previous thirteen Tests against West Indies, and Frederick Trueman, for one, saw no reason for that sequence to end. During the traditional team dinner on the eve of the first Test, at Old Trafford, Ted Dexter was, as usual, running through the opposition batsmen and their perceived strengths and weaknesses. Each evaluation was followed by a snort from Trueman and the promise that batsman 1,2,3 et cetera was wasting his time if he thought he could survive against Trueman's bouncer/yorker/leg cutter, etc. After a session of this double-act, Barrington interrupted to tell Trueman that he had plainly already reduced the West Indies to 12 for six and had better take a rest now or the match would be over inside three days.

Such bravado from Trueman was neither new nor specific to this series, but it was indicative of a general mood of confidence within Dexter's team. It did not last through the first match, however, because although there was, indeed, an early finish to the Old Trafford Test, it came about thanks to a display of overwhelming superiority by the West Indians, who amassed 501 for six declared before bowling out England for 205 and 296. Dexter's blazing 73, in the first innings, was a lonely act of defiance as, on a pitch taking increasing spin, Lance Gibbs wove his magic for match figures of 11 for 157. A week later, at Hove, West Indies dismissed Sussex for 59. If Dexter had any lingering doubts beforehand, he knew now what a formidable opposition he was pitched against. Consolation came through his own vibrant form. He failed, like everybody else, in that disastrous first innings at Hove but, in the second, he pummelled the West Indies attack for a century in only two and a half hours. It was the type of counter-attack for which few players have ever been better equipped. Dexter was to need, and use, such powers again at Lord's.

By now, he had seen quite enough of the touring side to realize that the prime quality required to bat against them was courage. He thought that Brian Close, 'the most fearless of the lot', should open the innings at Lord's but this idea was rejected. 'He may not have had the best technique against the moving, swinging ball,' recalled Dexter, 'but he knew how to defend both wicket and body against this very fast, but fairly straight bowling. I got Close into the side, all right, but did not manage to get him into the opening position.'

The other intriguing inclusion was that of Derek Shackleton, whose remarkably consistent wicket-taking for Hampshire had hitherto seen scant reward from the England selectors. Shackleton was now thirty-eight but had played only three Test matches, the last of them eleven years earlier in Delhi. His prolonged omission was credited to a general view that his bowling was too innocuous to be effective on Test pitches and against the best batsmen. Generations of county batsmen disputed this, perhaps including Dexter, whose own theory that Shackleton could be hit over the top, chronicled earlier, was proved wrong. Whatever, this was a notable international comeback, which probably surprised the mild-mannered Shackleton as much as anybody. Dexter said he wanted Shackleton's accuracy and his ability to bowl 40 overs a day. He put this fully to the test by giving him 84.2 overs in the game. The first thirty-eight were delivered on the opening day and failed to produce a wicket – vindicating those who had kept him out of the side all those years. But on the second morning Shackleton wrapped up the West Indies innings at 301 with three wickets in four balls, giving England cause for optimism.

This was instantly dissipated when John Edrich was out to the first ball he received, caught behind the wicket off Griffith. It was 2 for one, a pregnant moment for the captain to appear. But there was no pause, no hint of concern or restraint. Dexter was down the stairs, through the Long Room and on to the ground in near record time, adrenalin pumping as seldom before. 'I was quite certain as to what I was going to try to do. I had no intention of being an Aunt Sally for Hall and Griffith and I decided to strike back, top gear from the start.' Thus, one of the greatest of cameo innings was launched. Self-deprecatingly, Dexter says he was lucky to find his touch immediately. This was not luck; this was inspiration. *Wisden* called it 'a thrilling display of powerful driving, hooking and cutting . . . The way he stood up and punished the fiery fast bowling of Hall and Griffith was exciting to see.'

A still more graphic description was available on the airwaves.

John Arlott, by good fortune, was commentating for the early stages of the innings, in which Dexter reached 50 in only 48 minutes. His words to the nation, a nation agog by this time, are worth repeating: 'There is about Dexter, when he chooses to face fast bowling with determination, a sort of command that lifts him, or seems to lift him, above ordinary players. He seems to find time to play the fastest of bowling and still retain dignity, something near majesty, as he does it.' Later, in the same commentary, Dexter turned Hall to mid-wicket. Arlott purred with pleasure. 'It's another four. This takes Dexter up to 33 out of 47. Of course he's made bigger scores than 33 in Test matches and he may well do so this time. But I think I've never seen Dexter bat more assuredly or more commandingly and the situation he'd had to cope with immediately after lunch would have been a desperate one for any batsman in the world. He's risen to it, quite gloriously.'

When Dexter was out for 70, one of the finest 70s ever seen, England were 102 for three and still far from serene. Barrington, typically, and then Jim Parks and Fred Titmus all made crucial runs, however, and the total crept to 297, a deficit of only four runs. The game was wide open and this Test match was now occupying a disproportionate degree of conversation around the land. West Indies had fascinated people, for this was a new phenomenon. But England were taking them on, Dexter leading the counter-attack, and that was even better. On Saturday, the gates at Lord's were closed before the start, many who had queued since early morning being locked out. The fortunate ones saw another riveting day's play, Shackleton and Trueman reducing West Indies to 104 for five before Basil Butcher and Frank Worrell put on 110. Butcher's was the only century of the game but his team-mates largely wasted it on the fourth morning when the last five wickets went down for 15 in six overs.

Trueman was England's bristling hero now. He took 11 wickets in the match, equalling the West Indian pair for hostility, and certainly for skill, if not quite for speed. Much later, he revealed his private inspiration. 'During that match, when England were due to bat, I was having a quiet soak in one of the individual bathrooms at Lord's. Then I heard voices in the corridor outside. And I found myself listening to R.V.W. (Walter) Robins, chairman of the England selectors at the time, apparently talking to the two umpires about the suspect action of Griffith and the complaints which had been coming in from the various counties. I heard him say that the umpires should under no circumstances call Griffith for throwing. When they objected he explained that there was a lot of worry about racial tension in London and he feared a riot might be sparked if Griffith was no-balled at Lord's. When I came out of the bathroom Mr Robins was waiting for me. He had heard me moving about. He asked me if I had overheard the conversation so I had to admit that indeed I had. Then he solemnly asked me to give my word never to disclose it. I promised that I would keep silent for a time but told him that I thought it should be made public eventually if only to point out the handicap England had been playing under.' Trueman kept his word, honoured the silence, but took out his frustration on West Indian batsmen. 'I suppose in a way I benefited personally from the unfair situation . . . I became so angry that I found new reserves of strength.'

England required 234 to win and if this was not a mountainous target it certainly looked to be when three wickets fell for 31. This time, there was no majesty from Dexter, who was bowled by Lance Gibbs for just two. But Barrington, at the peak of his powers, defiant to the core, revelled in the situation, seeing off a barrage of short-pitched bowling by Hall and finding a like-minded ally in Close, who came in when Cowdrey retired to hospital. With a day remaining, England needed a further 118. Seven wickets were intact, though as Cowdrey's was among them this was effectively six. The last day promised drama on a grand scale, and rain and bad light delayed the start until 2.20 p.m., heightening the tension.

It had, already, been a strange game for Dexter. Though he perhaps scarcely felt it in the heat of battle, a blow he took from Griffith during his first innings had caused his left knee to swell.

He had been unable to field during the West Indies second innings and recalls the weird sensation of looking in upon the drama. 'I spent the time in the pavilion with my leg up and I sat there in a daze at the amazing goings-on.' Plainly far from fit, he batted in his usual position and suffered for it. 'My left leg had been strapped up with padding and I felt far from comfortable,' he confessed. Now, idle again, he fretted increasingly as that extraordinary final afternoon ran its course. His anxiety arose not only from the precarious state of the game and his deep desire to level the series but also from a profound belief that England were operating against unfair odds.

When he reflected upon this Test, Dexter said it was 'one of the most enthralling, exhausting, exasperating, heart-stopping games of cricket I ever played in. It shook the game, the country and it certainly shook me.' But when he reflected specifically on the final day, the emotions that sprang to mind were 'anger and despair'. He explained: 'Under the laws of the game, it would have been quite possible (and just) that neither Hall nor Griffith would have finished the day. One would have been off for throwing, the other for taking his time.' The West Indian over-rate in the closing stages was 14 per hour, which these days would almost win them a pat on the back for haste. But, as Dexter remarks: 'We could not see into the future that day. Wes Hall was taking a very long time to bowl an over. With defensive field placings, our task had been made very difficult.'

Close, who survived all the aggression, could not cope so manfully with the negative side of the West Indies' game. Bruised and battered about his body, he went bravely but bizarrely down the pitch – against Griffith of all people – and edged an ugly swing to leg. He was out for 70 with 15 still wanted but, now, numbers 10 and 11 were together.

The rest, of course, is part of cricketing folklore: 8 needed from the last over, then 6 from three balls before Shackleton was run out. Enter the wounded Cowdrey to stand at the non-striker's end while David Allen survived two balls from Hall. 'I was grateful Colin was not put to the test but I was bitterly disappointed we had not won a game which, I felt, we deserved to win,' said Dexter.

As it turned out, Lord's was the one match in the series that did not, for all its excitement, produce a positive result. England levelled the rubber in the third Test at Edgbaston, where the vengeful Trueman took 12 wickets and Dexter took four in an innings for only the second time in his Test career. But that was in the damp, dank conditions that the West Indians of the 1960s detested. At Leeds, three weeks later, the sun shone and England were crushed by 221 runs. They fared no better during a memorable finale at the Oval where, on the final day, the gates were closed on almost 24,000 people, roughly two-thirds of whom were West Indian. It was an unprecedented but fitting reaction to a milestone in world cricket.

There was a short tour to India that winter but Dexter chose to absent himself. His experiences in India two winters earlier had made a profound impression upon him and he was not drawn to return. He sought, instead, a rest from cricket to promote his varied business interests and to spend some time with Susan and their children, Thomas and Genevieve. M. J. K. Smith took over the captaincy but this was a temporary measure and Dexter, as expected, was reappointed for the 1964 home series. It was his last in charge, and, appropriately, it was against Australia. Not so appropriately, it was lost, so it remained one of the great regrets of his career that he had played in four Ashes series without winning one.

Benaud had retired and the Australian captaincy had passed to Bobby Simpson, as hard, shrewd and single-minded a man then as he has been, in latter years, as the influential coach of the Australian side. Other absentees included Alan Davidson and Neil Harvey, both probably celebrated by Dexter after the bad feeling generated two winters earlier. With eight of the touring party new to England, it was condemned by pundits on both sides of the world as one of the weakest ever to set forth on an Ashes tour. We have heard that one before and since, however. Dexter was no more taken in then than, much later, as chairman of selectors,

128

when similar disparagements were offered to the 1989 visitors. Both teams returned home in considerable triumph.

The 1964 series was disappointing, especially so when set in stark contrast to the vivid entertainment of the West Indies games the previous year. Four of the five Tests were drawn but the one that was not still haunts Dexter today. It took place at Headingley, where Dexter's strengths were already appreciated less than on other grounds, and was won for Australia by an innings of 160 by the pugnacious Queenslander Peter Burge. The controversy, which raged passionately for weeks afterwards, concerned Dexter's tactics against Burge, first in taking the second new ball when his two spinners had Australia on the ropes and then in overruling Fred Trueman on how he should be bowling, and to what field. The outcome was a fiasco and Dexter regretted it sharply. 'I left a deep footprint for the press to tread in for the rest of time,' he said graphically.

The point was that Australia, replying to England's modest 268, were in disarray at 178 for seven. Six wickets had gone down for 54 runs, three of them to Fred Titmus, and although Burge remained, unbeaten on 38, he had only the dregs for company when the new ball became due. It has widely been claimed that nobody in the ground expected Dexter to take off his spinners at that point but he saw it differently. In the ensuing seven overs, bowled by Trueman and Jack Flavell, Burge and Neil Hawke scored 42 runs and gathered the momentum to turn the game. They added 105 for the eighth wicket, Burge and Wally Grout put on a further 89 for the ninth and from facing a substantial deficit, Australia gained a decisive lead of 121. But, for all Burge's excellence, had they earned it? Or was it donated by Dexter's eccentricity?

From a distance, his tactic retains some logic. It is, after all, traditional to believe that tail-enders are more likely to be dismissed by quick bowling than spin and this was the straightforward Dexter plan. What he had not bargained for was that Trueman would be stubborn to the point of insubordinate, resulting in a quite absurd session of cricket that lost the match for England and, sensationally, lost Trueman his place in the team.

Trueman believed he could dismiss Burge on the hook. In other words, he would drop the ball short with a man set back behind square on the leg-side, waiting for the catch off a top edge. Dexter disagreed and declined to give Trueman the field he wanted. Trueman decided he would bowl short anyway. Result: shambles for England and free runs for Burge. 'Trueman', recounted *Wisden* with deep disapproval, 'fed him with a generous supply of medium-pace long hops.'

Unsurprisingly, Trueman has a different perspective on the episode. While acknowledging that many 'experts' regard this as the worst Test he ever played for England, he counters: 'But they don't know what was going on at the wicket. I blame Ted Dexter for what happened. He gave the impression he knew more about fast bowling than me.' Indignation has always sprung, readily as his pipe, to Trueman's lips but on this occasion he had his supporters, not least because when he did, at length, dismiss Burge, it was to a catch in the very position he had identified 122 runs earlier. This, however, could not pardon his deliberately contrary bowling, which was more futile than rebellious.

England lost that game by eight wickets and Dexter did not consider it one of the most satisfying experiences of his cricket life. It also irked him, more than he would admit, once again to be chasing a series against Australia. At Old Trafford, a fortnight later, it soon became plain that Simpson's strategy was to insure against defeat. This, he did phenomenally well. England, having lost the toss, did not take a wicket until the board read 201 and Simpson, who had opened with Bill Lawry, batted more than two days for his score of 311. He declared at 656 for eight, shortly before lunch on the third day but Dexter was intent that his team should not be cowed into submission. Ken Barrington later recalled how he 'issued orders of defiance' in the dressing room, before the England reply began and again at each interval. 'He was almost fanatically determined,' said Barrington.

If so, he could have had no more willing disciple than Barrington, who proceeded to make 256. With Dexter scoring

130

174, all prospect of a result was snuffed out and the teams reconvened at the Oval with Australia still 1–0 ahead. England recalled Trueman and Cowdrey, who had both been dropped for Old Trafford, but all chance of squaring the series vanished with a day's loss to rain and an inspired spell of bowling by Neil Hawke, which dismissed Dexter's team for 182.

Relations between Dexter and Trueman had been decidedly cool since the Headingley feud and there was a moment when they threatened to deteriorate further here. Trueman had begun bowling with 297 Test wickets to his name and he still had 297 by the time Australia had established a healthy first-innings lead. He had, in fact, bowled so inoffensively that it was small wonder Dexter did not instantly turn to him to have another go. Trueman, as ever, had other ideas. 'Just before lunch on the Saturday, I saw Ted standing at the wicket looking a bit vacant, ball in hand. I asked him what he was going to do and he said he was thinking of putting Peter Parfitt on to bowl. I said, "No, you're not", took the ball off him and put myself on.'

With his fifth ball, Trueman uprooted Ian Redpath's middle stump. With his sixth he had Garth McKenzie caught at slip. Hawke, his great friend, survived the hat-trick but duly became the 300th Trueman victim. Perhaps it could not be put down as an inspirational bowling change by Dexter, perhaps it is true he had little choice, but at least it all meant that there was something to be celebrated at the end of his last Test as England captain. Over a period of four years he had led England in 30 Tests. Nine had been won and only seven lost but, if the mark of a successful captain is to have won the major series, Dexter fell short. Even as he left the Oval, however, he was heading for another defeat, on an altogether different platform.

Chapter Ten

For a man who has often been labelled arrogant, Ted Dexter has a remarkable flair for self-deprecation. This will often come as a surprise to those who meet him, as it must surely have done in mid-1964 to the representatives of the Conservative Party who, in Ted's own words, 'knocked on my door and asked me to stand for parliament'.

'I told them I knew more about Italian politics than English but the sum total of both would not make up a five-minute speech to the Young Conservatives.' Such a scornful self-assessment would, under normal circumstances, have killed the notion at birth. That it did not was due to two factors. The Tories wanted a big name, a high-profile figure to help accelerate their pre-election bandwagon, and they had identified their target. And Dexter? Well, for him, it was the familiar tug of the unknown that overcame any rational objections. 'Here it was again,' he explained, 'this new experience, this challenge, this opportunity.' The truth was, he simply couldn't resist it.

But if, in one sense, this was Dexter the butterfly, seeking 'passing trade', as he likes to call it, for the sake of his own stimulation and interest, it did not come cheap. When the small print of the project was examined, it transpired that the date of the general election coincided precisely with the departure of the MCC team for the winter tour of South Africa. Dexter had visited South Africa with a Commonwealth side two years earlier but it was the one Test-playing nation he had yet to tour with England. It seemed a stark choice: sacrifice the remaining ambition of his cricket career, or give up on this political adventure.

The compromise pleased Ted. It meant that he had to surrender the England captaincy, though by then, perhaps, it had lost much of its attraction for him, but with the agreement of MCC and the England selectors, he was enabled to join the South African tour late, having first fought the seat of Cardiff South East.

Not everyone thought it a fine idea. By this time Neville Cardus was seventy-six years old, yet still wrote on cricket with an authority matched by few. He was unimpressed by the latest example of Dexter the dilettante, and said as much: 'It is beyond me that Dexter, a young man with his talents as a great cricketer, should think for a moment of giving up any of his days or nights to Westminster and politics.' But perhaps, in his heart, Dexter knew well that he would be giving up few, for he was planted largely as a publicity stunt, with no possible chance of finding himself an MP.

The constituency was one barrier. There was often an anguished cry from Glamorgan, in Dexter's days as chairman of England selectors, that he did not know his way across the Severn Bridge to watch their side. Much the same scepticism would have applied to his election campaign. What, it could reasonably be asked, did an England cricketer, born in Italy, based in London and representing Sussex, know about the social, industrial and economic problems of South Wales? Answers on a postage stamp, please . . .

But Dexter, with his charisma, might have overcome this, with Party help, if his opponent at the ballot box had been a lesser figure than James Callaghan. A rising star of socialist politics, and on course for 10 Downing Street, Callaghan was to become Chancellor of the Exchequer providing he held the Cardiff seat for Labour. And nobody, least of all Callaghan and his team, was in much doubt about that.

It was not difficult to see why the Conservatives should alight upon Dexter as a man to glamourize their campaign. He transcended cricket, even sport itself, as very few comparable sportsmen of his time could. His handsome features were probably thought likely to be good for some female votes and his popularity among commercial companies meant that his face was familiar even to those who had never attended a cricket match. A generation earlier, Denis Compton had become known as the 'Brylcreem Boy': for popularizing that hair product in a style it hardly deserved, Compton received a one-off payment of £750. Dexter, whose business activities were handled by an agent, Bagenall Harvey, had elevated the connection between sportsmen and selling to a new level. He advertised shirts, shaving cream and vermouth, which gained his face the awareness of a pretty wide cross-section of the public.

But while Dexter had a strong face and a good voice, he was not a naturally compelling orator. The same shortcomings of shyness and intolerance that have affected much of his life were evident again now, in a way described by his old Sussex mentor, Robin Marlar. 'People tended to laugh at Ted, rather than with him,' said Marlar, a man well used to the hustings himself, having contested the seat of Bolsover in the 1959 general election and North East Leicester in a 1962 by-election. Marlar was unsuccessful on both occasions and Dexter, he believes, was a preordained loser in Cardiff South East.

By the time he had completed the 1964 cricket season, once more with the reflected glory of Sussex winning the Gillette Cup, Dexter had relatively little time to prepare the ground in South Wales. He was possibly considered less of a risk factor, in this way, as his admitted ignorance of politics had some chance of remaining a matter between his conscience and his sponsors, but along the way there was, almost inevitably, an embarrassment or two. Dexter agreed to set out his manifesto, such as it was, at an election meeting in the city. The Callaghan team responded by planting one of their own men at the back of the hall, specifically to ask difficult questions over which Dexter would, understandably, stumble.

The episode seemed ill-conceived and it undeniably had the potential to be a polling-day disaster. In the event, the defeat Dexter suffered was honourable, for he attracted 22,288 votes against the 30,129 polled for James Callaghan. It was a sufficiently convincing victory to satisfy Labour but it had, after all, been seen as a safe socialist seat. Dexter could stand down with dignity intact as he retired from politics, one of his cluttered life's briefest diversions.

A more significant retirement was pending, for Dexter was entering the final few months of his career as a serious cricketer. Not that he was aware of it as he headed out to South Africa, late in 1964, still short of his thirtieth birthday and, by even the harshest assessments, still among the leading players in the world. Although this was to be the tour that completed his circuit of the Test countries, something he had set out to do, he did not, at the time, see it as a conclusion. No alternative to cricket was exercising any influence on him and, if pressed on the point, he might well have envisaged playing for a few further years. Certainly, he showed no sign of regret over the handover of the England captaincy. M. J. K. Smith took up the reins, just as he had in India a winter earlier, but now, for the first time, he had Dexter in the ranks beneath him. Smith recounts that there was never a problem with the change. 'Ted was just the same as ever, doing his own thing as always. I never found him difficult when he was captain and I certainly felt he was a good, straightforward man to have in my side.'

Oddly enough, Dexter captained MCC in his first match of the tour, Smith deciding to take the game off, and he demonstrated that the political sojourn had done him no harm by making 44 and 50 against a South African Colts side – an insignificant fixture but for the presence of Barry Richards in the South African side and the need, through mass illness, for the Colts to use six substitutes at one stage of the final day. He led the side once more in the prolonged run-up to the first Test but no envy or intrigue was involved. Some of those present, indeed, thought that Dexter seemed relieved to be rid of the job. Writing his tour account for *Wisden*, Basil Easterbrook commented that Dexter 'undoubtedly benefited from being relieved of the burden of captaincy. He seemed more relaxed and at ease than at any previous time in his career and made a major contribution to what was always an excellent dressing-room atmosphere.'

135

He performed in the middle, too, and despite finding some curious ways to get out, he averaged 57 in the Tests with a run aggregate second only to that of the indefatigable Barrington. At Johannesburg, two days before Christmas, he made 172 of an England total of 531. It was the last of his nine Test centuries and it completed his set of at least 100 against all six Test opponents.

England won the series, and Dexter returned home in late February, content with the prospect of leading Sussex, and not England, into a new home season. Content, yes, but possibly not animated. In hindsight, Dexter was prepared to admit that he had lost interest in county cricket prior to that season, which by definition made him an inadequate captain of Sussex. It was now that the players became alternately amused and irritated by his absences for apparently spurious reasons; allied to waning interest among the Sussex public, poor playing results and a ground at Hove now in desperate need of attention, there was reason aplenty for the dispirited dressing-room atmosphere that prevailed.

Dexter was still motivated by Test cricket, though quite how far his appetite had been sated perhaps even he was not immediately aware. The opening match of the split summer, divided between New Zealand and South Africa, was certainly not designed to enliven the tired palate. It was played at Birmingham, in unrelentingly cold, bleak weather, and watched over the five days by a total of only 21,000 people. England won by nine wickets but all reportage of the game was dominated by a turgid century by Barrington which resulted in him being dropped for the second Test at Lord's.

Dexter had not planned it this way, as we shall see, but Lord's in June, with the sun shining and runs there for the taking, was as good a way as any for it to end. It was another fairly uninspired match, New Zealand being comfortably beaten again, but the ceremony and tradition that accompanies every Lord's Test ensured it would be an occasion.

For nobody present was the occasion bigger than for John Snow. At the age of twenty-three, and after only one full season in the Sussex side, he was given his Test début, due recognition of a rare fast-bowling talent. He was not given the new ball, however. Fred Trueman's partner, when New Zealand batted first, was Fred Rumsey. Rumsey had taken the first four wickets cheaply by the time Snow was called upon to bowl but he plainly remembers his nerves, his naïvety at the top level, and the man who came to his aid. 'Ted talked me through my first spell and pretty much through the whole match,' recalled Snow. 'He stood at mid-off while I was bowling and had a word with me between deliveries. He simply kept encouraging me to bowl at off-stump. It probably didn't look much from the outside but his advice and obvious concern was crucial to me that day.'

Snow took two wickets in each innings. His county captain, having scored 62 in England's first innings, then won the game in the second as bad weather left England to make 152 in the last three hours of play. Dexter's unbeaten 80 gave the task an air of simplicity.

As usual, during the Lord's Test, Dexter had attended a party thrown by his schooldays' friend, Michael Martin. 'I had a house in St John's Wood in those days,' relates Martin, 'and the party became an annual tradition. I always felt it was a feather in my cap when Ted came along, even though we had been friends for so long.' But Martin had no suspicion that this was the last party he would give during Dexter's playing career. Neither, for that matter, did Dexter.

The day after the Test Match had ended so satisfactorily, Dexter was back at Lord's. The third-round draw in that year's Gillette Cup had given Sussex an away tie against Middlesex. It suited Dexter's purposes admirably, as he did not have to leave London and had only to shift his kit from the home dressing room, along the first-floor corridor to the visitors', but it marked a landmark in knockout cricket: Sussex's first defeat. Champions for the first two years of the competition's existence, Sussex had begun another defence in efficient fashion with a 58-run win over Worcestershire, who were in the process of winning the county championship for the second successive summer. Ten thousand people had flocked to New Road to watch that game and the general view was that Sussex were now clear of the greatest obstacle to a Gillette hat-trick. Middlesex proved otherwise, amassing 280 in their 60 overs to win by 90 runs. It was a chastening day for Dexter and, with a couple of free days before the next scheduled championship game, at Portsmouth, he was keen to get away from cricket and indulge his passion for horse-racing.

There was racing at Newbury on the Thursday, 24 June, and he was keen to go. Furthermore, he made arrangements with some racing friends to look at some horses, for he was now keen to join the ranks of the owners and race his own horse. It promised to be a diverting day. It was all of that, and more. Dexter enjoyed himself hugely. He was shown over some good-looking horses and at the races he backed a few winners and had a few drinks. By the time he climbed into his Jaguar for the drive back down the M4 to his Kensington home, he was in high good humour. But it was not to last. As he approached the London end of the motorway, he was aware that the petrol gauge was dangerously low. He pulled off down the slip-road towards Chiswick, knowing there was a garage within a few hundred yards, but even as he did so the car began to lose power. Two hundred yards short of the roundabout beneath Chiswick flyover the Jaguar gave a final apologetic cough and the engine expired. Dexter thought that there was a garage on the roundabout (he later discovered he had been mistaken) and began to push the car.

It soon became too much for him, so he decided to pull the car off the road and walk to the garage, where he could fill a can with petrol. It was 5.30 p.m., the peak of the capital's rush-hour, and as anyone who has been in that area of west London at such an hour will testify, manoeuvring a car is no easy matter even if you have an engine to help. Dexter, perspiring on the warm summer afternoon as he tried to heave his car backwards into a driveway, suddenly lost control. The vehicle accelerated away from him, but not before making heavy and damaging contact with its owner.

As the Jaguar smashed through the warehouse doors of the Martini Rossi building (another irony, for this was the arch-rival drink to the vermouth Dexter advertised), he realized he had not only made a monumental mess of the operation, he was also badly hurt. 'I had felt this sharp tug at my leg and when I looked down there was blood everywhere, gouging out of this colossal hole in it,' he described. 'I admit I was frightened.'

With a combination of shock, pain and immobility, Dexter lay down on the side of the teeming road, his head resting on a convenient post. Cars continued to stream past, their drivers either unaware of the drama being played out alongside them or, in that focused, blinkered way common to British road-users, interested only in their own deadline. It took a boy on a pushbike to give help. He stopped, sized up the situation, perhaps even recognized the prostrate form on the pavement. Then, telling Dexter he would summon an ambulance, he pedalled away furiously. Dexter never saw him again, never had the chance to thank him.

His leg was broken at the thigh and, by 9 p.m., he was undergoing a two-hour operation. It was a serious fracture and rehabilitation was long and uncomfortable.

Because of his celebrity status, more than his condition, the West Middlesex hospital was very strict about who could visit him, and when. Among those turned away was Gubby Allen, then the treasurer of MCC but, more importantly, according to Dexter himself, 'perhaps the greatest benefactor in my cricketing career'.

Bored with his confinement, irritable – because the leg refused to heal quickly – and subject to bouts of feverish sweating, Dexter at first amused himself by watching the tennis at Wimbledon on television. Once he had exhausted this avenue, he gave himself over to considering his position and took some far-reaching decisions. 'I had often thought,' he reflected, 'that I was going just that little bit too fast for myself and now here I was, at a dead stop on my back in bed. I realized in that bed that I had reached another turning point in my life. I had always thought it wouldn't be a bad thing to be rich and I knew I would get nowhere in that direction by staying on in the game until it gave me up.' He decided to retire from cricket but, maybe recognizing that he was not in the best circumstances to make such a serious decision, made no statement. He had every opportunity to do so, for apart from his weekly column in the *Observer*, he was also recruited to the BBC television commentary team for two of the three Test matches against South Africa, but he kept his own counsel until the matter could be deferred no longer.

The invitation to commentate, alongside Richie Benaud and Denis Compton, might have helped convince Dexter that he was taking a wise course, for it was apparent that a permanent opening could exist for him here. Between his two television engagements, he took a ten-day holiday on the Italian Riviera with Susan and their son, Thomas. After the final Test, the three returned to Italy along with daughter Genevieve, just fifteen months old. This time, they stayed with Ted's brother John, in his summer house near Menaggio. There, with the matchless view down Lake Como as a more calming force than the incarcerations of hospital and injury, Dexter decided that it should be all or nothing. If he was not going to tour Australia that winter – a decision he had already communicated to the England selectors – he saw nothing to be gained by hanging on to his job at Sussex, which many close to him believed he no longer approached with either passion or enthusiasm.

As soon as he returned to England, Dexter drove to Hove for an appointment with the chairman of Sussex, Arthur Gilligan. He told him that he was resigning from the captaincy and would be unavailable to play the following season. Both men believed that this would mark the end of Dexter's playing days but this proved not to be so.

From the public, who Dexter had attracted to cricket grounds in numbers that no other cricketer of his generation could claim, there was sorrow, when the news became official, that a man of barely thirty, and evidently still in his prime as a batsman, should so prematurely be lost to the game. Fellow players saw it differently. Robin Marlar, who had brought Ted to Sussex, identified him as captaincy material and rejoiced loudest of all when, through the Gillette Cup, his foresight was vindicated, spoke for most. 'It was no surprise to me at all that Ted retired when he did. He always said quite openly that he was only going to do one Test cycle, because he regarded it as no longer challenging to go through it all again. And county cricket without Test cricket would have held no appeal at all for him.' Dexter himself moved on with mixed feelings, of course, but the restless soul in him overrode any misgivings. And, as he said: 'The bills had to be paid.'

Chapter Eleven

If a harrowing evening beneath the Chiswick flyover and a more reflective period in a hospital bed gave Ted Dexter the message that it was time for him and cricket to part company, the follow-up line – what to do instead – was not so distinct. He was more fortunate than most cricketers in that there was family money to fall back upon, so the dole queue, undignified sanctuary for too many redundant sportsmen down the years, was never a factor. But he was still young and a man of unfulfilled ambitions. Idleness did not appeal; it was not in his nature. The ensuing few years, then, were, perhaps, a trial to him. 'I was not settled in any specific line of business,' he admits. 'There was some writing work, some television and the odd promotion to look after, but nothing constant. Free days were plentiful.'

These were the years in which the Dexter reputation as a dilettante was generously justified. He dabbled in a multitude of activities, settling in hardly any. His business could loosely be described as public relations, but it had developed no set direction and existed largely on client awareness of the Dexter name. It was as well that it existed at all, however, for, twenty-five years later, he confessed: 'It was the business that kept me in England. If I could have gone off to Monaco and played golf all year round, I would have forgotten all about cricket.' Yet because he was still on home soil and because he still loved the game, his links with cricket were sustained. At times they were tenuous and might easily have been broken but at others they were strong and significant, not to mention surprising. For instance, those who regarded Dexter as merely impetuous would have doubted he possessed the patience needed for committee work, but ever since his retirement as a player he has sat on any number of influential cricket committees – as a supplier of initiative and inspiration rather than as a reluctant figurehead.

Hardly had Dexter put his kitbag in the attic than he was elected to a committee charged with reforming the ailing English county game. It became known as the Clark committee, as its chairman was David Clark, a farmer who also chaired the Kent cricket committee. The Clark Report was the forerunner to the Palmer Report (headed by Charles Palmer) twenty years later, and the Murray Report (with Mike Murray as its spokesman) in 1992. The odd man out was Murray, in that he achieved the conversion of the reactionary counties, something neither Clark nor Palmer could manage.

The Clark committee formed a distinguished bunch: Dexter and Gubby Allen had captained England; Doug Insole, Brian Sellars and Stuart Surridge were former county captains; Ossie Wheatley and Fred Titmus were captains at the time. County administration was represented by Edmond King (Warwickshire), Geoffrey Howard (Surrey), Ken Turner (Northamptonshire), Mike Turner (Leicestershire), and the media by Charles Bray, a cricket correspondent for thirty years. The reason for the committee's being was the dramatic fall in popularity of championship cricket, which had attracted 2 million paying customers in 1950 and barely 500,000 fifteen years later. Everyone believed it was time for a change – until, that is, the committee presented its recommendations. Then everyone threw up their hands in horror.

Dexter had long been convinced that the county set-up was obsolete, that it encouraged complacency among players and boredom among spectators. He had said as much on many occasions, which was one good reason for including him on the reform committee. But after twelve meetings, embracing seventeen months of assiduous work, the Clark Report was thrown out by counties afflicted with the ostrich syndrome which, down the years, has retarded domestic cricket. Nothing can have dismayed Dexter more than the reaction of his own county, Sussex. Far from agreeing with the recommendation that the championship programme should be shortened and augmented with a new, limited-overs league, Sussex suggested there should be *more* first-class cricket.

The rejection was not only foolish but short-lived. By 1969 a one-day league was indeed operating with great success, while the championship programme has been steadily trimmed back over the years until four-day cricket, of which Dexter was a fervent supporter, took over in 1992. The message is that counties *will* change – but only at their own pace, rather than when someone else tells them what is best for them. It was this small-mindedness, as much as anything, that Dexter resented about the way the game was played, which might, on the face of it, make it still more surprising that he returned to the middle for a brief curtain-call in the summer of 1968.

It was not a promising scenario. Sussex were having a terrible summer under Jim Parks, heading for the championship wooden spoon for only the second time. England, now once more led by Colin Cowdrey, were struggling against an Australian side that did not begin to compare with their best of recent years. Perhaps it was the evident mediocrity that provoked Dexter's comeback. There was something of the shining white knight within him, and the idea that some still felt he could prosper at high level, after three years away from the game, would have appealed to his ego.

Robin Marlar, who also came out of retirement during 1968 'to play a few games for Sussex and see why there had been trouble with Parks as captain', believed the inspiration for Dexter's return was provided by Gubby Allen. Although no longer chairman of selectors, a position from which he had championed Dexter's cause, Allen continued to wield a mighty influence. 'He had been responsible for all manner of comebacks,' claims Marlar, 'including Cyril Washbrook in 1956 and David Sheppard in the early 1960s. England were losing in '68 and Gubby would have told Ted he was still required.'

John Woodcock, observing the developments as cricket correspondent of *The Times*, had a simpler explanation. 'Ted was missing the glory,' he said. Whatever the spur, Dexter was, doubtless, a welcome sight as he strolled into the Sussex dressing room at Hastings, in mid-July, for a championship match against neighbouring Kent. The team was at its lowest ebb. Although they were once more on the march in the Gillette Cup, heading for another final against Warwickshire, Sussex's championship form was dire and the team spirit almost non-existent. Parks, who had been such an effective deputy to Dexter – and the man with whom Dexter most enjoyed batting – was finding the burden of leadership all too onerous and the senior players were simply not responding to him. John Snow, now a prominent dressing-room figure and not always a force for peace, recalls many stories of unrest: 'There was not a good feeling in the dressing room and more than one story appeared in newspapers hinting of a player revolt during the early stages of 1968. Inevitably, my name was linked with some of the stories.'

Newer to the Sussex side, but destined to create still more controversy than Snow, was Tony Greig. He has no doubt that Dexter's return was the high spot of a dismal season. 'He could make the rest of us look the merest novices when he turned his mind to it,' said Greig. 'I remember the bustle of activity before the match at Hastings. I can't vouch for its authenticity but the story goes that our twelfth man was sent out from the ground to clear a runway of sorts so that Ted could land his private plane. When he strode into the dressing room, a strange smell accompanied him. It was his cricket case, unchanged after three years of semi-retirement and suffering severely from mould and dry rot.'

But, as both Snow and Greig admiringly recalled, there was nothing rotten about his batting. 'It was a helpful pitch for Derek Underwood, as Hastings usually was,' relates Snow. 'That was a challenge to Ted and he played him so well it was as if he had never been away. His natural flair saw him through and, in that one innings, he illustrated what rare ability he possessed.'

Greig was still more impressed. 'He gave Underwood hell. I have never seen him punished so severely, either before or since.

145

Ted even used the same old brown bat he had when he last played regularly. His presence made Sussex feel a team again. I have met few people who look the part of a cricketer quite as Ted did, and his stature brought confidence seeping back into the side.'

To make a century on comeback from three years of self-imposed exile would have been startling. To make a double, as Dexter did, was a towering achievement, quite one of the most impressive of his entire career. In its wake was generated such a newspaper clamour that the England selectors almost had their job done for them. Trailing Australia 1–0, with two Tests left, they would have been accused of dereliction of duty if they had ignored the former captain now being widely presented as a national saviour. The remarkable story gathered momentum and Dexter was included in the England side for the fourth Test at Headingley in July. Snow was with him, of course, and so too was Underwood. There were two England débutants, one of them the waif-like figure from rural Essex who later became team manager under Dexter's stewardship of the selectors. Keith Fletcher still shudders when he recalls his first Test, for he dropped two slip catches off Snow and was out for nought to general derision from a Yorkshire crowd irritated by the absence of their own Phil Sharpe. Dexter's return was a shade less humiliating and, unlike Fletcher, he retained his place for the final game of the series at the Oval. That, however, was both the beginning and the end of a career revived.

He did not do so badly. His scores in those two Tests were 10, 38, 21 and 28 – 97 runs in four innings. The first of the games was drawn and the second was won, due in large measure to the innings by Basil D'Oliveira, which was held up in ridicule of those who, with such disastrous consequences, left him out of the party due to tour South Africa that winter. The Oval match ended in high drama, with volunteers from the crowd helping to mop up the playing surface following a freak storm, and Underwood tying the Australians in knots in a way he had never managed to do with Dexter at Hastings.

Everyone involved emerged with their honour from the experiment. Dexter had made a few runs, vindicating the selectors, and England had levelled the series, delighting the public who had clamoured for his return. It had been a romantic story for a few, late summer weeks, but whether Dexter believed, in retrospect, that it had been a wise move is open to doubt. 'He didn't enjoy the experience,' says Robin Marlar bluntly. John Snow believes that Dexter had proved all he set out to, not least to himself, with the double century at Hastings. 'Afterwards, he may well have wondered if he wanted to carry on doing it. Certainly, I had the impression from the start that he would not be back with us for long.'

Dexter hardly bowled in the games he played and, when he did, it was a dispiriting experience. 'As I grew older, the elastic snapped,' he later reflected. 'I lost the pace, the zip and the sting had gone. I remember taking two catches off my own bowling against Glamorgan and being complimented on my cleverly disguised slower ball.' Conversely, his batting had largely stood the test of time. That he was out bowled in all four of his Test innings might indicate a rustiness in eye–hand co-ordination but at thirty-three he could, if he had wanted, have put that right with practice. The impression remains, therefore, that the comeback was never more than transient 'passing trade', more evidence, indeed, that he had not quite come to grips with life outside the cosy confines of cricket and cricketers.

Reflecting on his reasons for retiring in 1965, and the feelings that assailed him thereafter, Dexter explained: 'It is hard to give up, but it is best to give up when you are on top. I had had the complete package. I had played in over 60 Tests and captained England in more than half of them. I had been everywhere and what beckoned me was repetition. I left when I was winning but I missed it dreadfully and I have known others who have been lost completely when they could no longer play the game. Letting go is hard. I think it was the best part of seven years after I had stopped playing before I knew what to do with myself. You lose something in your life that can never be replaced, no matter how close to the game you stay.'

147

And Dexter stayed close. Apart from the Clark committee, he also sat on an MCC special sub-committee to look into the bane of throwing. He took no committee posts at Sussex but, in 1971, he even made a second, brief playing comeback to sample the delights of the John Player League. He also turned out when he could for his old school, Radley, in the Cricketer Cup.

His public-relations company, Ted Dexter Associates, inevitably brought him into regular contact with the game, because it reflected his own interests and many of these were cricket-connected. Some of his promotional schemes have been dismissed as hare-brained but others have been undeniably sincere and thoughtful. One such was the introduction of sponsorship for the touring team's games against the counties at a time when these fixtures were being increasingly devalued by the disinterest of the county teams and their habit of not fielding a full-strength team. Dexter brought in Holt Products to spice up the games with some prize money and, hey presto! the counties were suddenly interested again. That Tetley Bitter now pour larger sums of money into the touring itinerary should not cloud the issue: it was Dexter, long ago, who helped turn the tide.

The prompt for a number of his promotions was an underlying concern over playing standards in England. Hence, it was this that, many years later, in 1984, led to his nationwide Find-a-Fast-Bowler campaign. Dexter was dismayed that in thirty years, dating back to when he left Radley, he could name only five genuinely fast, Test-quality English bowlers. He included Brian Statham, Fred Trueman, Frank Tyson and John Snow alongside the man he recruited to help front the search, the recently retired Bob Willis. Their efforts had the sanction and blessing of the Test and County Cricket Board, and the curiosity of most of the country's cricket watchers, but as *Wisden* somewhat witheringly reported the following year: 'Nothing much came of it.' The promotion is now best known for Tim Munton – who bowled heroically throughout Warwickshire's record-setting 1994 – having been among the also-rans, though this is unfairly to denigrate a well-meaning project.

Speed has always been an obsession with Dexter, or so it would seem. He prefers to call the obsession 'quality'. 'I like quality in all things,' he says. 'I like watching the best in batting and bowling, and similarly I hanker after the best in other things, too.' These have included many modes of motorized transport, a fascination he may have adopted from his brother but was to take to far greater extremes.

John Dexter began collecting classic cars and motorcycles while still at school. Michael Martin, the Dexter family friend, recalls: 'At Radley, with the apparent knowledge and acceptance of the authorities, he kept a fine Salmson sports car and an Ariel motorbike. He liked to see himself as a figure of the 1930s and always wore the appropriate caps and clothes for this esoteric motoring.' John owned a long line of Bentleys (his favourite was nicknamed 'Betsy'), Jaguars, Alfa Romeos and Ferraris, and, says Martin, they were 'not always confessed to his family. When he took the wheel in one of these wondrous motor cars of the past he could have leapt from the pages of John Buchan, Dornford Yates or Sapper.'

Brother Ted followed suit, sharing the love of power and style on the road. But he went further, developing a passion for aviation. Never one for half measures, he acquired his own aircraft – a succession of them – obtained a pilot's licence and determined to fly himself around the world. He did not succeed in this without a few hair-raising experiences, which might have deterred a meeker man. The first came when he was flying across the Pennines to play for the International Cavaliers, for whom he still turned out on occasion. His plane was a Comanche, his passengers Peter Pollock, the South African fast bowler, and Deryck Murray, the West Indies wicketkeeper. 'The engine went sick and I had to put it down on the Yorkshire moors,' relates Dexter with casual regret. 'It was pretty inhospitable actually, but it could have been a lot worse. The plane was a write-off.'

The combination of golf and flying, passions in tandem, also lured Dexter into dangerous skies. He had just bought his first plane, a single-engined Falco with sleek Italian design to match its owner, and his enthusiasm to show it off at every opportunity was almost the end of him. He had arranged to play golf with Monty Court, a journalist friend on the *Sunday Mirror*, at Walton Heath in Surrey. This, however, was mid-winter and, on the morning in question, Surrey was cloaked in snow and frost. 'It did not take a moment', recounts Dexter, 'for my organizing brain and my flying ambitions to coincide. There might be no chance of golf in Surrey but I understood the weather was much better in the West Country. Why didn't we go down there for a game? Monty was half-way through an indignant plea that even he, golf addict as he was, did not intend to drive a 400-mile round-trip just for a game, when I slipped in the suggestion that we could go in the plane.'

When fired by an out-of-the-ordinary idea, Dexter sprouts animation. Never a man for dull routine, he is enchanted by the idea of diversions, whether they be to a race meeting, a cricket ground or dog kennels. 'All went well at first . . . we touched down at Weston-super-Mare, free of hazards, and were soon on the course at Burnham. If I was feeling self-congratulatory, however, it was a short-lived emotion. We played the first nine holes in reasonable weather but as we made the turn, so did the weather. Within a matter of minutes the skies had closed in ominously and greyness above had begun to produce rain, turning quickly to sleet and threatening snow at any time.

'When we took off again, Monty was looking apprehensive. He has since said that his pessimism was not lifted by the sight of my furrowed brow and my frequent tapping on the instrument panel. He didn't dare ask what was wrong but the engine was beginning to sound distinctly rough. I radioed ahead to White Waltham, our home airfield, and received bad news. The weather there was too bad for us to land. I tried one or two other airfields, nearby, without luck, so took the only remaining option and decided that we must head back to Weston. The weather was now appalling and the Falco had begun to struggle badly but we made it safely, booked into a hotel and headed straight for the bar for a much-needed restorative. In England, the one consolation about weather of such severity is that it very seldom lasts beyond a single day and, true to form, we were able to fly back to Waltham in relatively balmy conditions the following morning, none the worse for one of the pieces of golfing organization on which I cannot entirely look back with pride.'

He can, unquestionably, look back with pride upon his round-the-world flight. He had planned it meticulously, aiming to combine it with covering the 1970–71 cricket tour of Australia for his newspaper. As part of the training process for the mission, Ted successfully applied to crew an entrant in the London to Sydney air race the previous year. This venture, however, ended in distress. 'I got as far as Karachi and went down with pneumonia,' he explained. 'I was stuck there in a hospital bed while the race went on without me.'

When it came to the real thing, Dexter's ambitions went beyond piloting himself to Australia and back: he intended to take his wife and two children, too. According to friends, Susan was not daunted on her own behalf, even if she was for the children. 'Susan was as intrepid as Ted,' says Michael Martin. 'When Ted went out on his powerful motorbikes, Sue would don her leathers and ride behind him. She was as keen as he was on the flight to Australia.' And so, after Martin had given them a farewell party, the Dexter family set off in October 1970.

By Dexter standards, it was a smooth, uneventful journey. Ted and Susan sat up front, Tom and Genevieve behind, and by a series of hops across Europe and Asia, half the world was conquered in ample time for Dexter to report on the first Test of the Ashes-winning tour captained by Raymond Illingworth.

Dexter, by now, had traded in his column on the *Observer* for a more lucrative, though somehow less suitable post as cricket correspondent of the *Sunday Mirror*. He continued to write for that paper until cricket administration reclaimed him in 1989 but whether, in the years that followed, he wished he had worked elsewhere is open to conjecture. Certainly, the tabloid press had a ready answer whenever Dexter complained of their hectoring tactics: he had long been one of them.

His heart may have remained on the *Observer*. Certainly, some of his friends did, and when Dexter branched into a new line of country in the mid-1970s, writing a novel, he enlisted the help of his long-time sports editor on the paper, the late Clifford Makins. Dexter and Makins combined on two books, *Testkill* and *Deadly Putter*. It hardly needs saying that their backgrounds were cricket and golf respectively, but these were not soft, sentimental tales, they were racy, rollicking and sometimes randy accounts of dubious morals and desperate murders. *Testkill*, at least, was critically well received. It was immensely readable, the cricketing stage set with the touch of one who knows his subject intimately, and if, in the book's hero, Jack Stenton, there was more than a touch of Dexter himself, so much the more fascinating. He almost owned up on page one:

My name is Jack Stenton. I captained my county and played for England. I batted first wicket down and scored my share of runs at a time when there was a vintage crop of fast bowlers to cope with. Like some other first-class cricketers I turned to journalism to write a column for a national daily newspaper. My background was comfortable and conventional . . . I was a public schoolboy and learned my cricket by a combination of good coaching, good wickets and strong competition . . .'

The autobiographical note was not sustained throughout the book, but by putting himself in the shoes of Jack Stenton, Dexter applied some self-assessments to the plot, as well as some cricketing insights available only to the privileged few.

Trawling the sensations of his own playing days, now a decade removed, Dexter was employing his greatest strengths and transmitting them to the reader. Again, later in the book:

It is commonplace that the Monday morning of a Test match normally suffers its share of the weekend hangover. There is none of the pent-up, pin-drop atmosphere of the first session on a Thursday. Batsmen, bowlers, fielders, even the captains, take quite a time to adjust to the existing tactical situation.

The voice of one who knows, one who has been there and felt it. Here was Dexter, using his own experiences in tandem with his fascination for the technical and psychological sides of the game. It was part autobiographical, part coaching-manual, and yet, used in context, it gave the novel an authentic feel. Perhaps he should have kept Jack Stenton to cricketing matters; when he brought him back, suddenly transported to a golf setting for *Deadly Putter*, it did not work so well. Dexter might even have become the Dick Francis of cricket fiction, but he would never have had the patience and single-mindedness with which Francis researches and writes a novel each year, always to the same rigid timetable, always to formula, always a best-seller. Dexter never could devote himself so exclusively to a single-item agenda; his mind would forever have been wandering on to new territories. After two books, he ceased to be a novelist.

His business life was by now established, a directorship or two running parallel with the day-to-day promotions of the public-relations company, the weekly column for the *Sunday Mirror* and his continuing commentary work with the BBC. There, in the television commentary box, there was a regular pre-play ritual in which the *Sporting Life* was spread on the desk, and Dexter, Richie Benaud and Jim Laker would exchange opinions and information about the afternoon's racing. All three were regular punters, Dexter usually wagering the biggest sums but not always pocketing the most frequent winnings. He had fulfilled his ambition of horse ownership, without conspicuous success, and his business life was seldom so congested that he could not make time for an afternoon's punting at Sandown Park, Windsor – in striking distance of both home and office at Ealing – or one of his more rural favourites, Fontwell Park in Sussex. He would often go alone, giving himself and others only a few moments' notice, but he was not averse to company. More than once, when I had arranged to meet him, he would soon be peering speculatively at his watch, drawing in his breath and proposing: 'We could just catch the second race at Windsor. Do the business in the car on the way.' There is within him this desire for escape, and his features always light up when the office is left behind and he has pointed the Jaguar (or whatever it is) in the direction of the racecourse.

The contradictions of Dexter are best bound up in this side of his life. Here we have an elegant, impeccably bred fellow, who once admitted that a friend had called him 'too aristocratic for royalty', utterly at his ease in the throng of the common man, amid the jellied eels and cast-off betting tickets of the silver ring. And it is not only horses that intrigue him.

Greyhounds cost much less than racehorses, both to purchase and to train. They can also be raced far more regularly, sometimes as often as once a week. Dexter went into this in grand style, at one stage owning a number of dogs outright and making frequent trips down the M4 to their training kennels in the flightpath of Heathrow airport, a bleak, functional place but, for Dexter, the breeding ground of carefully hatched plans. He liked to involve himself in the programme mapped out for each dog and, inevitably, his aim in each case was not only to win races but to pursue the ever elusive coup in the betting ring. In the hunt for this, Dexter could be observed on some remote and ramshackle dog tracks, the type that attract twenty spectators to each of two bookmakers, as well as the viewing restaurant at the Wembley dog meeting each Saturday night. He is as comfortable incognito, in flat cap, as in top hat or trilby. Anonymity and solitude suit him fine.

Wembley became a ritual, surviving the years. Family and friends would often join the Dexter party and the excitement would, naturally, be heightened if one of Dexter's dogs was running. Among the group, more than once, was the rector of the Dexters' local church in Ealing, who had become a close friend of the family and, clearly, enjoyed his night of sport like everyone else.

Gambling was, for a time, a big thing in Ted's life but, paradoxically, no bigger than religion. 'Ours was a strong Church of

England family but, as so often happens, I had lost touch with the church during my playing career. During the 1960s, Susan and I were both very taken by Billy Graham, the evangelist, and I think it was after we had gone together to watch him one evening that we became what is known as born-again Christians. I began to see more of David Sheppard and I did speak from the pulpit once, at a sportsmen's service, but in general I just took on the Church as an increasingly important part of my life.'

It is typical of Dexter that he never mentions quite what an integral part of his local church he became, and how much time, effort and money he put their way. In the Church, as in cricket, the good works of Dexter escape general attention. Suffice it to say that both he and Susan became pillars of the Church community in Ealing, supporting every function, attending almost every Sunday and generally achieving the reputation of people who could be relied on.

Chapter Twelve

The trimmings of fame and glamour that attached themselves to Ted Dexter during his playing career were largely absorbed by retirement. He remained a public name but an essentially private personality, a discreet man most unlikely to be found embroiled in the type of tabloid scandal that has, in recent years, claimed sportsmen of similar profile. By his own design and determination, too, the troubles that periodically affected his family remained their property alone. They were observed, of course, by close friends such as Michael Martin, who is in no doubt about the quality which has guided Dexter through all domestic strife. 'First and foremost, he is a very kindly fellow. If you had a problem, he would help you. Ted is one of the very few people in the world I would turn to if I was in trouble.'

David Dexter, the youngest of the three brothers, has unwittingly but undeniably placed emotional and financial strains on the family but, where the reaction of some would be an ignorant shame and of others an ostentatious patronizing, the Dexters have borne their tragedy with evident love and dignity. Douglas Birks, master at Radley in the time of Ted and John, recalls how David, their Down's syndrome brother, would sometimes be brought by their parents for a cricket or rugby match. 'Both Ted and John were very good with him, perfectly natural in what might have been a difficult situation,' said Birks.

When the parents could do no more, Ted took over. David was educated in the Sheiling Creative School for Backward Children and, at the height of his fame as a player, Ted went to speak at the school and learn more about their teaching methods. Later,

David was moved to a Care Home but holidays were spent with one or both of his brothers.

If an extra input of stability was needed in the Dexter household, Susan generally provided it. Dexter has never made any secret of his pride in Susan, that marrying her was the best day's work he ever did, a view shared by their close friends. Michael Martin, who enjoyed 'innocently taking her out when Ted was away playing cricket', describes Susan as 'a star girl, an extremely nice person and a great influence on Ted'. That she was also a popular addition to cricket's social circuit is confirmed by John Snow. 'I remember going to quite a few parties at Ted's house. They were generous hosts, great fun to be with, but most of the guys would go weak at the knees when Susan was about.'

When the Dexter name is mentioned, the imaginings of many would turn to a lifestyle of sunshine socialites. This has not often been the case, other than when the clan gathered in Italy, at the summer home of elder brother John. His villa, above Menaggio and surrounded by the mountains of the Trepontine Alps, was open house to family and friends during the sunshine months, and the Dexters would sail, swim, wine and dine in style and luxury.

In 1962, John had married Ann D'Arcy Smith, affectionately known to her friends as D'Arcy, and they made their home in Milan, where John was a shooting star of Italian business. He was twice chairman of the Chamber of Commerce for Italy, finance director of the British Institute in Florence, and he founded and chaired the board of the foremost English-speaking school in Milan. He has three daughters – Lucy, Camilla and Juliet – who, naturally enough, spent many of their childhood holidays with the offspring of Ted and Susan.

As so often with the son of a gifted and famous father, Tom doubtless felt much was expected of him and, perhaps, even resented it. He did follow Ted and John to Radley, one of those routine expectations, but he was never quite up to the academic demands of such a school and he soon left to complete his education elsewhere. Genevieve grew up with a father who doted upon her but it was quickly obvious that she had an independent, if not rebellious streak. An early, innocent example dates back to a Gaudy (former pupils' reunion) at Radley in the late 1970s. Genevieve, then thirteen and wearing an elegant long dress bought specially for the occasion, went missing during the afternoon and was discovered, with another girl of similar spirit, riding bareback on some ponies they had rounded up – in a nearby field.

The popular image of Dexter, as a man for whom life has never been difficult, is hopelessly flawed. His children gave him sleepless nights, just as other people's children do. There had been a good deal for him to worry over during those years. In 1974, shortly after they had returned to England to live, both his parents died.

If he needed escapism, or peace of mind, Ted's route would habitually take him down the A30 to Sunningdale Golf Club. He had become a member at Sunningdale early in his cricket career and it played a steadily increasing role in his life's routine once he had hung up his boots.

It is well chronicled that Dexter had the ability to have pursued a career in golf, rather than cricket, less well chronicled that he is now relieved he did not. While cricket consumed most of his waking hours, golf was a recreation to be enjoyed, and he had time only to squeeze in a round when it was convenient. But when golf became his only active sport, the competitor within Dexter began to weigh up his game in a different light. Playing off scratch meant that he was an exceptional club golfer, well able to beat almost anyone at Sunningdale. But could he hold his own at the higher level? The question began to gnaw at Dexter's ever restless mind until he could stand it no longer – which is why, at forty-two, he shelved his business life to become a tournament golfer for a year.

In anyone else, this might have been thought irrational, if not irresponsible. In Dexter, it was seen as characteristic and intriguing. People expected him to do the unexpected; they also had a sneaking suspicion that he would do rather well. As for the family, well, their reaction was all that he expected: 'When I told them what I had decided, they automatically dismissed it as another of my passing fads. They know how often I am briefly taken by an idea, only to discard it quickly as the fascination fades. But this one I carried through to the end.'

Dexter played for a year on the European amateur circuit. 'I was keenly conscious of the fact that I badly wanted to find out where I stood in the golfing hierarchy before it was too late. There was only one way. For one year, golf had to supersede everything. I had to practise more diligently than ever before and play tournaments every week.'

'I had assessed the prospects as clinically as possible. My own game, I felt, could stand the test of all the amateur tournaments Britain could offer. I might not win many but I would hold my own. The thing I had always found striking, and in many ways rather depressing, was the gulf which existed between the good golf professional and the household name, not to mention the similarly vast discrepancy in the other direction, between the good pro and the average club player. I felt I could be better than the average club player, if not as good as pros. It was that which I gave myself this year to prove.'

It was the summer of 1978 and Dexter was contracted to the *Sunday Mirror* as a cricket writer. Before setting out on this latest project, he had divest himself of this commitment. This achieved, he awarded himself leave from his own company and went to Portugal for practice and pro-am tournaments in warm weather and on dry courses. 'By the time the serious stuff began I was in pretty good shape, mentally and physically.'

'The year was by no means a riot of garlands and glory,' reflected Dexter, 'but it was far from being a disaster, either. I had my share of success.' The greatest of these came on a springtime Saturday at Deal, in Kent, when he won the Prince of Wales Cup, a prestigious event for leading amateurs. This gave him renewed heart for the ultimate aim of this extra-curricular year, which was to qualify for the Open Championship at St Andrew's in July. The qualifying rounds were all played on nearby Scottish courses and, said Dexter, 'I was playing well enough at the time to feel I had a chance of taking one of the qualifying places.'

He began his final round at Leven, with a clear idea of the score he needed for one of the coveted Open places. 'Leven is a typical links course, not unlike St Andrew's itself. It has large, undulating greens and is not too punishing to the wayward shot. But, as so often in that part of the world, wind was the enemy, a fierce, howling wind which picks up your golf-ball and performs cruel tricks with it. I battled against the elements, kept my head above water and turned downwind with a few holes to go, well aware that I had a very clear chance of qualifying.' Having played the sixteenth and seventeenth to par, Dexter came to the last knowing that a four would suffice. Nerves began to churn for, despite the deadpan, iceberg appearance, he is not above tension. He struck his tee-shot well enough but then, as he relates, 'The worst possible thing happened. I had been staying with an amateur golfer who lived near the course, a well-meaning but nervous sort, and he chose this of all moments to appear at my shoulder. I wanted to see no one on that walk down the fairway to my ball, least of all my flustering friend.' As the unwelcome host hovered distractingly, Dexter got away with a four-iron approach and a difficult pitch. 'I didn't hit it well but it ran to within six feet of the hole. Six feet, separating Dexter from that dream of lining up with Nicklaus and the rest. Here I was, one stroke from the achievement that would have satisfied my private golfing ego, perhaps for ever. I kept my head down and still, my legs firm, and struck it cleanly. I was convinced it was straight but at the last, dreadful split-second it faded, catching the lip of the hole and spinning out.'

Dexter now had to take part in a sudden-death play-off but, all passion spent, it was a cruel extension of agony and, soon, 'I was trudging off feeling grim and tired, having allowed my game to fall apart. When I finally reached home, the reaction really set in. The clubs went into a cupboard, like a naughty schoolboy in disgrace, and there they stayed for the next six months.'

Despite the instant dismay, it had been a considerable performance by Dexter to reach the threshold of his ambition, for not only was the tour a one-off dalliance, he was also of an age that, by all sporting logic, put him some way past his peak. The standard of

160